J. Paul McCutcheon
THE LARCENY ACT 1916

THE ROUND HALL PRESS
IRISH STATUTES ANNOTATED SERIES

General Editor: Tony Kerr

1   *The Larceny Act 1916:* J. Paul McCutcheon

The Larceny Act 1916

J. Paul McCutcheon.
BCL, LLM, Assistant Lecturer-in-Law, NIHE Limerick

THE ROUND HALL PRESS

The typesetting for this book
was output by Gilbert Gough Typesetting, Dublin,
for the Round Hall Press,
Kill Lane, Blackrock, Co. Dublin

BRITISH LIBRARY CATALOGUING IN PUBLICATION DATA
McCutcheon, J. Paul
1. Ireland (Republic). Law. Theft
I. Title
344.17'05262

ISBN 0-947686-18-5
ISBN 0-947686-17-7 Pbk

Printed in Great Britain by
Billing & Sons Ltd, Worcester

Contents

Foreword

The text of a statute, as every lawyer knows only too well, is merely the starting point on one's quest for the law on a particular topic. Sections will have acquired a coat or two of judicial gloss. Some the courts may have struck down on constitutional grounds. Other sections may have been repealed or inserted by subsequent amending legislation. Consolidation statutes are rarely to be encountered. Occasionally the search is impeded by the fact that the relevant statute predates the founding of the State and thus may not be generally available. Indeed the only pre-1922 legislation obtainable through the Government Publications Sales Office is the Sale of Goods Act 1893 and the Merchandise Marks Act 1887. Moreover the statute, though still in force here, may have even been repealed in its entirety by the United Kingdom parliament.

The Larceny Act 1916 is a case in point. It is thus an appropriate statute to lead off The Round Hall Press's, *Irish Statutes Annotated* series. It is a statute which has generated a considerable accretion of case law, of which there has been no prior comprehensive treatment. It has also been amended in a number of important respects without being the subject of consolidating legislation.

This new series provides the complete up-to-date text of the Act, incorporating all subsequent amendments and noting any delegated legislation, coupled with an authoritative section-by-section commentary analysing the relevant case law. The series will not be confined, however, to pre-1922 legislation nor will it necessarily be confined to legislation which has undergone considerable amendment, as the second title in the series — the Civil Liability Act 1961 — demonstrates.

As it develops the series aims at filling a small but significant gap in Irish legal literature. In the meantime suggestions for future titles will be gratefully received.

Anthony Kerr
University College Dublin

Tables

References are to paragraph numbers.

ARTICLES OF THE CONSTITUTION

TABLE OF STATUTES

TABLE OF CASES

Tables, with reference to paragraph numbers

Introduction

Background to the Larceny Act

1   The Larceny Act 1916, as amended, which amounts to a codification of the Irish law on dishonest appropriations, must be seen as the product of eight centuries of legal evolution. Concepts and principles which shaped the medieval law continue to influence the modern law. The development of the law is characterised by judicial articulation of common law standards, accompanied by legislative reactions thereto. Many of the offences contained in the Act are legislative creations, enacted in response to judicial circumscription of the offence of larceny.[1]

2   Larceny became a felony when it was included by Henry II amongst the Pleas of the Crown to be prosecuted on indictment.[2] It was defined by Bracton as being "the fraudulent dealing with another man's property with the intent of stealing it against the will of the owner".[3] Central to the offence was an unlawful interference with possession; there had to be a trespassory taking and carrying away of property. If the taking was not trespassory it was not larceny. A number of consequences flowed from that proposition. If the property was obtained with the consent of the owner there was no larceny, regardless of what happened thereafter. Thus, bailees and servants could not be convicted of stealing property given to them by their bailors or employers. If the owner gave a real consent to the taking it was immaterial that it was obtained by deceit. Moreover, a person in possession of property enjoyed the rights of ownership unless and until they were displaced by a superior right. Accordingly, a third party who knowingly acquired property from a thief was not guilty of felony.[4] On the other hand, not all trespasses amounted to larceny; the felonious nature of the taking was determined by the intent of the

1   E.g. embezzlement, obtaining by false pretences, receiving.
2   Assize of Clarendon (1166). See generally Stephen, *History of the Criminal Law of England*, Vol. 3, pp. 121-176; Holdsworth, *A History of English Law*, Vol. 3, pp. 360-370; Pollock and Maitland, *History of English Law*, Vol. 2, pp. 494-500; Fletcher, "The Metamorphosis of Larceny" (1976) 89 Harv.L.R. 469; Weinreb, "Manifest Criminality, Criminal Intent, and the 'Metamorphosis of Larceny'" (1980) 90 Yale L.J. 294.
3   Cited in Holdsworth, *op.cit.* p. 360.
4   Receiving was made a felony by 5 Anne c.31.

1

accused at the time of the taking. A further requirement was that the stolen property have some value. Initially this was taken to mean that the property should be of some material use, and property which was merely decorative or ornamental was not the subject of larceny. Eventually, it became settled that property of any economic value, however slight, could be stolen.[5]

3   In order to amount to larceny the interference with possession required a taking and carrying away, and it followed that a misappropriation of land was not larceny; land by its very nature cannot be taken and carried away. This principle was extended to things which savoured of realty, such as title deeds and things attached to land. Moreover, things which were not in the possession of anybody, or which could not be in anybody's possession, could not be stolen. Consequently, abandoned property and wild animals were not the subject of larceny. An additional reason for the exclusion of wild animals was that they were considered to possess no value when in their natural state.[6]

4   The offence of larceny, therefore, was narrowly defined, and many dishonest appropriations fell outside its scope. Apart from the exclusion of realty from the subjects of larceny, any transfer of possession by the owner, even though deceitfully obtained, took the misappropriation beyond the frontier of larceny. A consequence was the perception of problems in the cases of dishonest bailees and servants to whom goods were delivered by the owners. The courts dealt with those issues by focussing on and refining the concept of possession.[7]

5   The first major judicial extension of the law of larceny occurred in *The Carrier's Case*.[8] There a carrier who broke open bales of goods, given to him by a merchant, and appropriated the contents thereof was held to be guilty of larceny. The problem facing the court was that the carrier had been given possession of the goods by their owner and, therefore, it did not appear that there was a felonious taking. However, the argument which prevailed was that of Chokke J, namely that the carrier was given possession of the bales and not the contents, and the taking of the contents was held to amount to an acquisition of possession. The rule which emerged from the case was that a bailee

---

5   See Stephen *op.cit.* p. 137.

6   Stephen refers to the case of a man who was summoned for being in unlawful possession of a crocodile *op.cit.* p. 163.

7   See Beale, "The Borderland of Larceny" (1892-3) 6 Harv.L.R. 244.

8   (1474) YB Pasch. 13 Edw.4 f.9 pl.5; 64 Seldon Society 30.

who "broke bulk"[9] and misappropriated goods was guilty of larceny, whereas the bailee who misappropriated the entire bale was not. It was not until 1857 that Parliament brought all bailees within the scope of larceny.[10]

6   With regard to servants the doctrine developed that goods entrusted by a master to a servant remained in the master's possession as long as the servant was on the master's premises or in his presence.[11] In 1529 Parliament supplemented this by enacting that servants were amenable to larceny in respect of all goods entrusted to them by their masters.[12] This was later explained on the theory that possession did not pass to the servant.[13] Nevertheless it would appear that, if the goods were given to the servant for a special purpose, possession passed.[14] Different considerations arose where a third party delivered goods to a servant on behalf of the master. In *R v Bazeley*[15] it was held that the master did not acquire possession until the goods were placed in the proper repository. If, instead of placing them there, the servant took the goods it was not larceny, as there had been no interference with possession. Thus, a servant who pocketed coins instead of placing them in the cash drawer was not guilty of an offence. In response to that decision Parliament, in the same year, created the offence of embezzlement.[16]

7   At the same time, however, the courts displayed a willingness to hold that goods collected by a servant for his master were in the possession of the latter, by employing a doctrine of constructive possession. In *R v Reed*[17] the accused collected coal on behalf of his master and placed it in the master's cart. On the journey to the master's premises he disposed of some of the coal. He was held to be guilty of larceny, on the ground that his exclusive possession of the coal

9   I.e. committed an act which determined the bailment.

10 Prevention of Frauds Act 1857, s.4.

11 Coke, *Third Inst.* 108 (1506). Likewise, goods given to a person on licence by the owner were considered to remain in the possession of the latter. For instance, cutlery and plates used by a diner in an inn remained in the possession of the innkeeper.

12 21 Hen.8 c.7.

13 *R v Bass* (1782) 1 Leach 251; see also *The State (Foley) v Carroll* [1980] I.R. 150, 153-4.

14 See Holdsworth *op.cit.* p. 365.

15 (1799) 2 Leach 835; see also *R v Waite* (1743) 1 Leach 28.

16 39 Geo.3 c.85.

17 (1854) Dears. 168, 257.

determined when the coal was placed in the cart, and the master acquired constructive possession. Had the accused taken the coal before placing it in the cart he would have been guilty of embezzlement, not larceny.[18]

8   A related development was to restrict the cases where an owner, who physically handed over goods, would be held to have parted with possession. In essence, the courts created a distinction between physical possession, or custody, and possession for the purposes of the law of larceny. In *R v Chisser*[19] it was held that goods given by a shopkeeper to a customer for inspection remained in the former's possession. Thus, the customer who absconded with the goods was guilty of larceny. A more radical development was the creation of larceny by a trick in *R v Pear*.[20] There the accused hired a horse for a particular journey, and, instead of returning it, sold it. The jury found that the accused originally intended to sell the horse, and that, at the time of hiring, the journey was a pretence. On those facts the English Court for Crown Cases Reserved held that larceny had been committed. The delivery of the horse did not alter the nature of the possession, which remained in the owner until the time of the conversion. The proposition stated by the judges was that where possession has been parted with, but the owner did not intend to part with property in the goods, and the possession was obtained by fraud, a subsequent conversion amounts to larceny.[21] What was crucial to the decision was the accused's intention, at the outset, to convert the goods once he had obtained custody of them. Where an accused did not have a felonious intention at the time of delivery, a subsequent conversion of the goods was not larceny.[22]

9   In general, however, the acquisition of property by fraud or by means of a fraudulent breach of trust did not amount to an offence at common law. Cheating was a common law misdemeanour which consisted of defrauding by means which were injurious to the public

18 See also *R v Abrahat* (1798) 2 Leach 824; *R v Spears* (1798) 2 Leach 825.
19 (1678) T.Raym. 275. In *R v Colhoun* (1840) 2 Cr. & D. 57 the accused who absconded with, and appropriated the contents of, a parcel entrusted to him to deliver was held to be guilty of larceny. Although he was not a servant of the owner, the case was treated as being similar to such a case, and possession was deemed to remain in the owner.
20 (1779) 1 Leach 212; see Beale *op.cit.* note 7 *supra*.
21 However, if the prosecutor intended to part with property in the goods no larceny was committed; *R v Parkes* (1794) 2 Leach 614.
22 *R v Banks* (1821) Russ. & Ry. 441.

generally, such as the use of false weights or measures. In the absence of such means no offence was committed, and the acquisition of property by means of a false representation was immune from sanction until 1757, when obtaining by false pretences was made a statutory misdemeanour.[23] With respect to breaches of trust, the offence of embezzlement did not apply to trustees or agents, it being confined to clerks and servants. Consequently a number of statutory offences of a limited nature were created which put fraudulent breaches of trust by certain agents on the same footing as embezzlement by servants.[24] Trustees in whom the legal interest of the property was vested were not brought within the scope of the criminal law until 1857.[25] The more general offence of fraudulent conversion was created by the Larceny Act 1901.

10 Burglary was a common law offence which involved the breaking and entering of a dwelling at night with intent to commit a felony. In essence the offence was a violation of the sanctity of the dwelling. The related offence committed during daytime was housebreaking. Robbery was larceny aggravated by violence and was a felony from the time of Henry II. Extortion was related to robbery. Several eighteenth century statutes provided for the punishment of attempts to extort money by letters threatening to accuse persons of crimes.[26] The extortion of money by a verbal threat to accuse the prosecutor of unnatural practices was held to be robbery.[27] Threatening with intent to extort was later made a statutory offence.[28]

11 The Larceny Act 1861 was the first consolidation of the law of larceny and related offences in Ireland.[29] Curiously the Act, which consisted of one hundred and twenty-three sections, did not define larceny nor did it deal with any of its underlying doctrines. Instead, it contained many copiously-detailed exceptions to the common law rules on larceny of animals,[30] documents,[31] and things attached to or

23 30 Geo.2 c.24.
24 E.g. 52 Geo.3 c.63; 7 & 8 Geo.4 c.29 ss.49 & 51.
25 Prevention of Frauds Act 1857. Bailees were also brought within the scope of larceny by the statute.
26 9 Geo.1 c.22; 27 Geo.2 c.15; 30 Geo.2 c.24.
27 *R v Jones* (1776) 1 Leach 139; see also *R v Pollock and Divers* [1966] 2 All E.R. 97.
28 4 Geo.4 c.54
29 An earlier consolidating act, 7 & 8 Geo.4 c.29, applied in England only.
30 Ss. 10-26.
31 Ss. 27-30.

part of the land.[32] In addition, it provided for larceny by bailees[33] and aggravated forms of larceny.[34] Related offences dealt with were robbery and extortion,[35] burglary and housebreaking,[36] embezzlement and criminal breaches of trust,[37] obtaining by false pretences,[38] and receiving.[39] The remainder of the Act dealt mainly with procedural matters. The bulk of the Act was repealed by the Larceny Act 1916.

12   The Larceny Act 1916 is considerably less cumbersome than its predecessor, its object being to "consolidate and simplify" the law of larceny and related offences. Unlike the 1861 Act, it contains a definition of stealing. Section 2 provides for the punishment of simple larceny, whilst sections 3 to 16 deal with other forms of larceny. Other offences contained in the Act are embezzlement,[40] fraudulent conversion,[41] robbery, burglary and aggravated burglary,[42] demanding with menaces,[43] obtaining by false pretences[44] and receiving.[45] The Act also deals with jurisdictional and procedural matters. The Act became part of the law of the Irish Free State, and later part of the law of Ireland. It follows that, with the exception of post-1937 amendments, it does not enjoy the presumption of constitutionality.

32 Ss. 31-39.
33 S. 3.
34 Ss. 60-66.
35 Ss. 40-49.
36 Ss. 50-59.
37 Ss. 67-87.
38 Ss. 88-90.
39 Ss. 91-99.
40 Ss. 17-19.
41 Ss. 20-22.
42 S. 23, inserted by ss. 5-7 of the Criminal Law (Jurisdiction) Act 1976. The offences of robbery, burglary, and aggravated burglary were amended to bring them into line with the equivalent Northern Irish offences. Although the operation of the 1976 Act was not dependent on uniformity of these offences in the two jurisdictions, the Law Enforcement Commission suggested that the respective legislatures might consider it desirable; see *Law Enforcement Commission Report* Prl. 3832, p. 22.
43 Ss. 29-31.
44 S. 32.
45 S. 33.

Larceny and Possession

13   As stated earlier, larceny is essentially an offence against possession, not ownership, of goods. It must be established that the accused removed the goods from the possession of the owner with the intent at the time of taking to deprive the owner permanently. The fundamental principle is that an innocent taking does not become larceny on a subsequent intentional appropriation. It is not surprising, therefore, that the courts have devoted much attention to the central concept of possession and its violation.[46] It should be remembered that originally larceny was not categorised as an offence against property. Rather, its principal concern was with the protection of public security and the general communal sense of well- being.[47] It was this public dimension, manifested in the requirement that the taking be by stealth or force, which brought the offence within the scope of the criminal law. The violation of possession which this entailed concurred with the collective image of a thief. Where, however, possession was voluntarily transferred the matter was essentially a private transaction which fell within the scope of the civil law. The immunity conferred by possession was the expression of an implied norm, which Fletcher has called that of "objective criminality".[48] The one exception where possession did not confer immunity on the accused was where a bailee "broke bulk".[49] In other words, by focussing on possession the law required proof of an act which coincided unambiguously with the general impression of thief-like conduct. Thus, the law incorporated a distinction between theft and dishonesty; although all larcenies were dishonest, not all dishonesty was larceny. However, as concern with dishonesty grew the perspective adopted altered accordingly. The history of larceny is one of its development and extension, through refinements of the concept of possession, to include certain dishonest appropriations. In particular, the courts refined, or redefined, possession in a manner which increasingly brought dishonesty within the scope of larceny. This was supplemented by the statutory creation of offences like embezzlement, fraudulent conversion and obtaining by false pretences which

---

46 See Edwards, "Possession and Larceny" (1950) 3 Current Legal Problems 127.

47 See Fletcher, "The Metamorphosis of Larceny" (1976) 89 Harv.L.R. 469.

48 *Ibid.*, 476-481.

49 *The Carrier's Case* (1474) 64 Seldon Society 30; see para. 5 *supra*.

represented a parliamentary response to the deficiencies perceived in the law of larceny and the concept of possession.

14   Possession is not a concept which is unique to larceny and certain broad comparisons can be made with other areas of the criminal law. A fundamental distinction which is drawn is that between custody and possession. Custody consists of a physical holding of goods whereas possession suggests an element of control. A person can possess goods without their being in his custody.[50] Likewise, a person who has custody of goods does not necessarily have possession of them. In *Minister for Posts and Telegraphs v Campbell*[51] Davitt J equated control and possession where he said that a person cannot possess goods unless he has control of them either personally or by someone else. Where a person exercises physical control over goods he is in actual possession of them and where control is exercised through a third party possession is constructive. Moreover, a person is in possession of goods only where he is aware of their existence. In the course of his judgment Davitt J referred to an earlier decision of the Court of Criminal Appeal, *The People (Attorney General) v Nugent and Byrne*.[52] In that case the two accused were charged with receiving stolen money which was found in a car owned by one of them and in which both of them were travelling. In allowing their appeals the Court held that there was no evidence from which knowledge of the existence of the goods could be inferred. As regards the passenger a further ground for allowing the appeal was that there was no evidence that he exercised control over the car or its contents. In *The People (Attorney General) v Kelly and Robinson*,[53] also a receiving case, it was held that the accused was in possession of goods which were in the hands of a third party where he retained some control over them; the accused could call for the delivery of the goods at any time. The two features which distinguish possession from custody are control and knowledge of the existence of the thing which it is alleged was possessed. In respect of containers it is possible that the accused could

---

50 See *Sullivan v Earl of Caithness* [1976] Q.B. 966 where the accused was held to be in possession of shotguns which were located in his mother's house, his mother being held to have "custodial possession" only; see also *Hall v Cotton* [1987] Q.B. 504.

51 [1966] I.R. 69.

52 (1964) 98 I.L.T.R. 139; 1 Frewen 294.

53 (1953) 1 Frewen 147.

be in possession of the container but not its contents where he is unaware of the existence of the latter.[54]

15   However, when applied to larceny the concept of possession becomes a minefield of technical distinctions which are difficult, if not impossible, to reconcile. The required coincidence in larceny of the taking and the intent created difficulties where the accused decided to appropriate goods after he innocently acquired custody of them. If the acquisition of possession coincided with an innocent acquisition of custody a subsequent conversion of the goods is not larceny. A number of rules developed governing the acquisition of possession by those who have custody of goods. Thus, an inn-keeper retains possession of the plates and cutlery used by his guests and an employer retains possession of goods which he gives to his employee.[55] Initially the goods are merely in the custody of the guest or employee and possession is acquired when they are subsequently appropriated, which usually will be accompanied by the necessary intent. Those rules can be explained by the obvious retention by the inn-keeper or employer of control over the goods which is sufficient to keep them in his possession. Where, however, goods are delivered to the employee on his employer's behalf, the latter does not acquire possession unless they are placed in the proper repository; until then the goods are in the possession of the employee.[56] Whilst it is difficult to see why the employer is in possession of the goods in one case but not the other the distinction is well-established and beyond dispute.[57] It could be said that, in symbolic terms, the act of placing the coins in the cash register unambiguously brings them within the dominion,

---

54 See *Warner v Metropolitan Police Commissioner* [1969] 2 A.C. 256.

55 Coke, *Third Inst.* 108 (1506); para 6 *supra*; see also *R v Chisser* (1678) T.Raym. 275.

56 *R v Bazeley* (1799) 2 Leach 835.

57 However, to add to the confusion it has been held that a servant who was given goods by her employer and which were forcibly taken from her had a "special property" which was sufficient possession to sustain an indictment for robbery; see *R v Harding* (1929) 21 Cr. App. R. 166. As robbery is essentially larceny aggravated by circumstances of force it would appear to follow that the servant would have had a sufficient possession for the purposes of larceny. But had the servant appropriated the goods she would have been guilty of larceny as the goods are deemed to be in the possession of the employer! In *Smith v Desmond* [1965] A.C. 960 it was not contended that an employee did not have a special property sufficient to found a charge of robbery of his employer's goods. It is submitted that in that respect *Harding* ought not to be followed by an Irish court. It should be noted that when the case was decided the force required to

or control, of the employer and puts the question of his possession beyond doubt.

16 Possession was further refined by the development of larceny by a trick and larceny by finding. The problem in both cases is that the initial acquisition of the goods is apparently innocent. The development of larceny by a trick was achieved by postponing the acquisition of possession until the goods are converted.[58] The accused's fraudulent intent at the time he acquires the goods prevents the owner's delivery of them from passing possession. If, however, the accused does not acquire the goods with fraudulent intent, possession passes and a subsequent conversion is not larceny.[59] With regard to larceny by finding the accused acquires possession at the outset, but that acquisition is a "taking" due to the accused's knowledge at that time that the true owner could be located.[60] In both cases the time at which possession is acquired is determined by the accused's state of mind in respect of the goods; the fraudulent intent or the knowledge that the owner can be traced are the crucial elements in determining the accused's guilt. However, the accused's mental state acts to delay the acquisition of possession in one case and to ensure that it coincides with the acquisition of custody in the other.

17 A related development occurred in *R v Riley*.[61] There the accused placed his flock of sheep in a field with the owner's consent. When he collected them the following morning one of the owner's sheep joined his flock and was driven off with them. The accused, unaware of this, did not discover the extra sheep until he came to sell the flock. At that stage he decided to appropriate the additional animal. His conviction was affirmed on the ground that the initial taking of the sheep was trespassory, not innocent. The later disposal of the sheep with intent was sufficient to amount to larceny. In *Ruse v Read*[62] the accused took a bicycle when drunk, cycled it for some time and, when

establish robbery had to be directed to the person who possessed the goods, which would explain the court's zeal to find that the servant was the possessor. Under the amended section 23, the force required can be directed towards "any person". Thus, an accused, in similar circumstances, would be guilty of robbery even though the employer retains possession of the goods.

58 *R v Pear* (1779) 1 Leach 212.
59 *R v Banks* (1821) Russ. & Ry. 441.
60 *R v Wynne* (1786) 1 Leach 413; *R v Deaves* (1869) I.R. 3 C.L. 306.
61 (1853) Dears. 149; see Turner, "Larceny and Trespass" (1942) 58 L.Q.R. 340.
62 [1949] 1 All E.R. 398.

sober, he brought it with him to his lodgings. The following morning he panicked and dispatched the bicycle by rail. At the time of the initial taking of the bicycle the accused's drunkeness precluded him from forming the requisite intent.[63] However, one of the grounds advanced by the Divisional Court for upholding his conviction, was based on *Riley*. Although his initial taking was not felonious, the accused's possession was a continuing trespass and the later formation of intent completed the larceny. However, to constitute a continuing trespass the initial taking must be wrongful, in the sense of its being wilful or negligent.[64] But in *Riley* it could only be said with a long stretch of the imagination that the taking was negligent, much less wilful. Rather the accused's taking of the sheep was inadvertent and should have been regarded as innocent. Likewise if in *Ruse v Read* the accused's intoxication was sufficient to prevent the formation of *mens rea* it presumably made his taking of the bicycle inadvertent. The question has not arisen in Ireland and it is submitted that those decisions should be rejected on the ground that the initial takings were not trespassory. However, the question remains whether a taking which is truly trespassory can become larceny on the subsequent formation of intent. For instance, could a joy- rider who later decides to appropriate the car which he trespassorily took be convicted of larceny? A basis on which a conviction could stand is to consider the trespass to be a continuous act which merges with the *mens rea* to complete the offence.[65] However, that would be to extend artificially the act of taking which in reality occupies only an instant. The joy-rider takes the car when he acquires possession by entering it; it could hardly be said that the taking is still in progress two and a half hours (and a police car chase) later. Moreover, it does not follow from the proposition that all larcenies involve a trespass that any trespass can become larceny. The larcenous nature of the taking is

---

63 See *D.P.P. v Beard* [1920] A.C. 479.

64 See *E.S.B. v Hastings & Co Ltd* [1965] Ir. Jur. Rep. 51; see McMahon and Binchy, *The Irish Law of Torts* (Abingdon, 1981), p. 537.

65 In *Fagan v Metropolitan Police Commissioner* [1969] 1 Q.B. 439, the Divisional Court held that the accused's conduct could be regarded as a continuing act which was accompanied by *mens rea* formed after the conduct began but before it ceased. In *R v Miller* [1982] Q.B. 532 the Court of Appeal applied the continuing act theory to arson. The House of Lords, [1983] 2 A.C. 161, upheld the decision but on a different basis, being on the view that the accused was under a duty to act; see Smith [1982] Crim. L.R. 527, 773; Glanville Williams [1982] Crim. L.R. 773.

determined by the fraudulent intent at the time possession is acquired.[66]

18   Greatest difficulty has been experienced where the owner has delivered goods to the accused under some mistake. In *R v Middleton*[67] a post-office clerk inadvertently overpaid the accused by placing the money on the counter. The accused who noticed the mistake collected the money and made off with it. His conviction of larceny was confirmed on the ground that the accused, when he obtained the money, was aware of the mistake and had formed the necessary intent. What was crucial to the decision was the accused's awareness of the error at the time he collected the money. In *R v Ashwell*[68] the accused, who sought to borrow a shilling from the prosecutor, was given a coin which neither realised at the time was a sovereign. On subsequently discovering the mistake the accused appropriated the coin. His conviction of larceny was affirmed by the English Court for Crown Cases Reserved, the judges having divided evenly on the question. Lord Coleridge CJ, who favoured upholding the conviction, argued that possession may only be transferred by "intelligent delivery". As both parties were initially ignorant of the coin's being a sovereign, possession did not pass and the accused only acquired possession when he became aware of the coin's value. However, by that time he had formed the intent which, therefore, coincided with the taking and the accused's conduct amounted to larceny. In words which were to be quoted in later cases he said:[69]

> In good sense it seems to me [the accused] did not take it till he knew what he had got; and when he knew what he had got, that same instant he stole it.

Stephen J, on the other hand, considered that view to be a fiction designed to evade the principle that a fraudulent appropriation subsequent to an innocent taking is not larceny. The distinction between the two cases is important. Whereas both cases involved the mistaken overpayment of money, the time at which the accused acquired possession differed. In *Middleton* the accused acquired

---

66 See para. 2 *supra*. See, however, *Minigall v McCammon* [1970] S.A.S.R. 82 where the South Australian Supreme Court applied *R v Riley* to a finder of goods.

67 (1873) L.R. 2 C.C.R. 38.

68 (1885) 16 Q.B.D. 190; but see *R v Flowers* (1886) 16 Q.B.D. 643.

69 *Ibid.*, 225.

possession at the time of delivery because, by being aware of the mistake, he had formed intent. In *Ashwell*, however, the acquisition of possession did not coincide with delivery, but was delayed until the accused became aware of the mistake.

19   In *R v Hehir*[70] the Irish Court for Crown Cases Reserved had to consider the same question. The accused was given a £10 note which both he and the deliverer believed at the time to be a £1 note. The accused later discovered the error and decided to appropriate the money to his own use. The majority refused to follow *Ashwell* and overturned the conviction. They held that the accused acquired possession of the money when the packet was delivered to him and, since that acquisition was innocent, his subsequent conversion did not amount to larceny. Between the time of delivery and the discovery of the mistake the accused had lawful possession of the money. *Ashwell* was considered to be a weak authority which overlooked the distinction, made in *Middleton*, between possession and property.[71] Palles CB accepted Lord Coleridge's view that there must be an "intelligent delivery". That requirement, however, is satisfied once the parties are aware of the existence of the goods.[72] A mistake as to a particular quality, into which category the majority considered the note's value to fall, did not negative the transfer of possession. Several questions were, however, left unanswered by *Hehir*. The distinction between the existence of a thing and its qualities is not altogether clear. Presumably a mistake as to a quality could be of sufficient magnitude as to make the thing substantially different from that which it was believed to be.[73] If existence is to be equated with nature a belief that the thing delivered is something completely different would be a mistake as to its existence. If that is the case, the mistaken delivery of a currency note, where both parties believe it to be a lottery ticket, would not effect a transfer of possession. The deliverer in *Hehir* intended to give the accused a currency note and that is what was delivered; the mistake was as to the value of the note which was one of its qualities but did not alter its nature. Nevertheless, *Hehir* remains the leading Irish authority on the point and, in the light of more recent

70 [1895] 2 I.R. 709.
71 *Ibid.*, 753.
72 *Ibid.*, 755.
73 An analogy exists in the law of contract where a mistake as to the quality of the subject matter of the contract might be of sufficient magnitude that the thing delivered is different in nature from that which it was believed to be; see *Bell v Lever Brothers Ltd* [1932] A.C. 161.

English decisions, its rejection of *Ashwell* is important.

20   The English cases which have been decided after *R v Hehir* display a degree of confusion which the Irish courts have been fortunate not to have encountered.[74] In *R v Hudson*[75] the accused was mistakenly sent an envelope which, when he opened it some time later, he discovered to contain a cheque drawn in favour of "Hudson". He returned the cheque to sender with a request to insert his initial on it, and the sender complied. The accused then had the cheque paid into his bank account and later withdrew from it. His conviction of larceny was upheld by the Court of Criminal Appeal. Relying on the words of Lord Coleridge, quoted above,[76] the Court held that he did not obtain possession of the cheque until he opened the envelope and became aware of it, at which time he also formed intent.[77] In *Moynes v Coopper*[78] the accused, who had received an advance on his wages, was mistakenly given the full amount. Neither he nor the wages' clerk realised the error at the time. On opening his wage packet the accused discovered the mistake and converted the extra money. His conviction of larceny was quashed by the Divisional Court on the ground that the clerk intended to give him the money, whereas in *Hudson* neither the envelope nor the cheque were intended for the accused. *Hudson* was followed in *Russell v Smith*[79] where the accused converted eight extra sacks which were mistakenly loaded onto his truck. *Moynes v Coopper* was distinguished on the ground that the accused in *Russell v Smith* was not intended to get the additional sacks. Once again the court held that the accused did not acquire possession until he knew what had been delivered to him. Likewise, an additional ground advanced in *Ruse v Read*[80] for upholding the accused's conviction was that he did not acquire the bicycle until he became aware that he had it, at which time he formed intent.

---

74   See Edwards, "Possession and Larceny" (1950) 3 Current Legal Problems 127; Carter, "Knowledge, Ignorance and Animus Furandi" [1959] Crim. L.R. 613.

75   [1943] 1 All E.R. 642.

76   See para. 18 *supra*.

77   See *contra R v Mucklow* (1827) 1 Mood. C.C. 160; *R v Davies* (1856) Dears. 640. In both cases the accused were held not to be guilty in circumstances similar to *Hudson* on the ground that possession of the contents was acquired when the accused first received the letter.

78   [1956] 1 All E.R. 450.

79   [1957] 2 All E.R. 796.

80   [1949] 1 All E.R. 398.

21   The effect of those decisions is to postpone the time that possession
is acquired from delivery to the time that the accused becomes aware
of the mistake. The conclusion to be drawn would appear to be that
the accused acquires possession on delivery only if the deliverer
intends, albeit mistakenly, to give him the goods. Moreover, it would
appear that the deliverer must intend to give him the full amount. In
Moynes v Coopper the clerk intended to give the accused the full
amount of his wages, without deduction. In *Russell v Smith*
presumably the loader intended to give the accused a certain number
of sacks; what he did not intend to give him was the eight additional
sacks. And in *R v Hudson* it was not intended that the accused get
either the envelope or the cheque. Where it is not intended that the
accused gets the goods he does not obtain possession until he becomes
aware not only of the existence of the goods but also their quality. In
Russell v Smith the accused knew that he had sacks on board his truck;
what he did not know was that he had the extra sacks and it was those
which he did not possess until he became aware of their presence. It
is submitted that those decisions are inconsistent with *R v Hehir* and
ought not to be followed. There is no difference between believing
£10 to be £1 and believing X + 8 sacks to be X sacks. In either case
the deliverer decides to give a particular quantity but mistakenly gives
a larger amount believing it to be the smaller.[81] Moreover, the English
decisions were based on the judgments in *R v Ashwell* which favoured
upholding the conviction, which judgments were rejected in *Hehir*.
In one respect, however, were the facts of *Hudson* to arise in Ireland
it might be possible to hold that the accused does not acquire
possession of the cheque until he discovers it on opening the envelope.
It is possible that an accused can possess a container yet not possess
its contents if he is ignorant of the latter.[82] Thus, where he is unaware

---

81   In *Hehir* Palles CB saw no difference for the purpose of the decision between
a £10 note and ten £1 notes.

82   *Warner v Metropolitan Police Commissioner* [1969] 2 A.C. 256. In *Merry v
Green* (1841) 7 M & W 623, a civil case, the purchaser of a bureau without its
contents was held not to have acquired possession of money which was
concealed in a secret drawer. The court assumed for the purposes of argument
that the bureau was sold on the express condition that he was not to have title
to the contents. It is submittted that even in the absence of such a term the
purchaser would not have acquired possession of the money as he was ignorant
of its existence. However, in *Minigall v McCammon* [1970] S.A.S.R. 82, 91 it
was suggested that a finder who takes physical custody of a thing capable of
containing something has possession of the thing and its contents sufficient to
support a civil action in trespass.

that a cheque is enclosed he would not acquire possession until he learns of its existence. However, where he is aware of the existence of the enclosed thing and is merely mistaken as to its quality the accused would acquire possession.

22   With regard to possession and knowledge matters are further confused by decisions to the effect that a prosecutor can acquire possession without his knowing of the existence of the goods. In *R Rowe*[83] a company was held to be in possession of iron which had fallen, or had been thrown, into its canal despite its ignorance of the iron's existence. In *R v Foley*[84] Gibson J stated that goods which are abandoned on a person's land fall into the "constructive possession" of the landowner.[85] However, it is by no means apparent that the landowner was aware of the existence of the goods in that case. It could be that those decisions are confined to circumstances where goods are deposited on land and there is no superior right to their possession. But it does not require an unduly cynical perspective to note that the attitude of the courts seems to vary depending on whether the question is one relating to the prosecutor's title or the accused's guilt.[86] Indeed the English cases decided after *Hehir* reflect a desire on the part of the courts to ensure the conviction of dishonesty even at the expense of judicial consistency. It has been suggested that the difficulties presented by the English cases could have been avoided by charging the accused with fraudulent conversion.[87] That, however, presupposes that an overpaid accused assumes a fiduciary responsibility towards the owner of the goods.

Larceny and Fraud

23   A correlation can be identified between the development of the doctrine of possession and the desire to punish dishonesty. The history of that development is one of the doctrine's being remoulded to

83   (1859) Bell C.C. 93.
84   (1889) 26 L.R. Ir. 299.
85   *Ibid.*, 301; in *Hibbert v McKiernan* [1948] 2 K.B. 142 it was held that lost golf balls which were abandoned by their owners on a golf course were in the possession of the golf club; see also *Webb v Ireland*, [1988] I.L.R.M. 501; *Parker v British Airways* [1982] Q.B. 1004.
86   Edwards, "Possession and Larceny" (1950) 3 Current Legal Problems 127, 145; Carter, "Knowledge, Ignorance and Animus Furandi" [1959] Crim. L.R. 613.
87   Edwards *op.cit.* pp. 150-151; see paras 88-89 *infra*.

incorporate a variety of dishonest appropriations. On the other hand, the accused is not guilty where the appropriation was not fraudulent.[88] In comparison to the multitude of cases on possession cases on fraud are few. Despite that, fraud is, as O'Byrne J remarked in *The People (Attorney General) v Grey*,[89] the outstanding characteristic of many of the offences which are contained in the Larceny Act 1916. Through the use of expressions like "fraudulent", "fraudulently" and "intent to defraud" fraud is central to the major offences in the Act. Moreover, the expressions "steal" and "intent to steal" import the element of fraud from the definition of stealing in section 1.

24   The classical definition of fraud is that of Stephen who wrote that:[90]

> Fraud involves, speaking generally, the idea of injury wilfully effected or intended to be effected either by deceit or secretly. It is essential to fraud that the fraudulent person's conduct should not be merely wrongful, but should be intentionally and knowingly wrongful. . . . Fraud is inconsistent with claim of right made in good faith to do the act complained of. A man who takes possession of property which he really believes to be his own does not take it fraudulently, however unfounded his claim may be.

This passage was cited with approval by the English Court of Criminal Appeal in *R v Bernhard*,[91] which was followed in *Grey*. In *Bernhard* it was held that a claim of right was a defence to a charge of demanding with menaces with intent to steal;[92] that intent is referable to the definition of "steal" in section 1 which includes the words "fraudulently and without claim of right made in good faith". Moreover, the claim made need not be one that is recognised by law, the sole requirement being that the accused honestly believed the claim to be justified. Thus, the accused's claim which was based on an unenforceable contract negatived the required element of fraud. Likewise the accused's belief in *The People (DPP) v O'Loughlin*[93] that he was entitled to remove goods in order to enforce payment of a debt which was owed to him was held to be good. Claim of right is

---

88 See Arlidge & Parry, *Fraud* (London, 1985); Edwards, *Mens Rea in Statutory Offences* (London, 1955) ch 8.
89 [1944] I.R. 326.
90 *History of the Criminal Law of England*, Vol 3, p. 124.
91 [1938] 2 K.B. 164.
92 See para. 141 *infra*.
93 [1979] I.R. 85.

available as a defence to offences which are defined as being fraudulent or which require an intent to steal.

25   In most cases fraud is negatived by a claim of right on the part of the accused. However, in some instances the accused might attempt to negative fraud not by a claim of right but by some extra-legal standard. It has been suggested that a person who mistakenly picks up goods, believing them to be his, is not guilty of larceny, as his conduct is not fraudulent; his mistake of fact precludes fraud on his part.[94] But that mistake could also be categorised as a claim of right in that the accused is honestly asserting a right of ownership in goods which are not in fact his.[95] However, cases might arise where no claim of right is involved yet it is argued that the taking is not fraudulent because it is not dishonest and does not attract moral opprobrium. For example, an employee might take money from his employer's cash register as a temporary, albeit unauthorised, loan intending to repay it at a later stage. In that case claim of right might not be available as a defence, especially where the employer expressly forbade such conduct. Moreover, the taking is likely to be based on a belief that the employer would not object to it were he aware of the circumstances, rather than on an asserted right. In other words, the employee's conduct is premissed on a belief that it is not dishonest, rather than on one that it is lawful. The question, therefore, is whether fraud (or any of its cognates) simply refers to an absence of a claim of right or whether it bears a wider meaning. If the narrower meaning is to be adopted it would follow that only a claim of right would negative fraud even though the taking might not be condemned by society as being dishonest.

26   In *The People (Attorney General) v Grey*[96] O'Byrne J noted that fraud is a concept common in both the criminal and civil law. Although he declined to provide an exhaustive definition he considered fraud to refer to something dishonest or morally wrong, particularly the acquisition of a material benefit by unfair means.[97] These remarks appear to support the attribution of a meaning to fraud which is wider than a mere absence of a claim of right. They suggest that fraud is to be equated with dishonesty and that the issue should be tested in the light of prevailing social standards of conduct. Thus,

94 Edwards, *Mens Rea in Statutory Offences* (London, 1955), p. 183.
95 *Ibid.*
96 [1944] I.R. 326.
97 *Ibid.* 332.

the question whether the accused acted fraudulently would principally be one of fact to be determined by the jury drawing on their experience of those standards. On the other hand, there is some authority to the effect that an accused acts fraudulently where he does not exercise a claim of right. In effect, it is suggested that the word "fraudulently" adds nothing to "without claim of right" and that, in this respect, it is redundant.[98] Thus, once the accused is aware that the taking is unauthorised it is deemed to be fraudulent. It is interesting to note that the English Theft Act 1968 replaced the expression "fraudulently" with "dishonestly". In *R v Feely*[99] Lawton LJ suggested that "fraudulently" had acquired a special meaning as a result of case law.[1]

27   The issue has been considered in some recent English cases. In *R v Williams*[2] the accused were shopkeepers who also ran a sub-post office. In order to finance their business, which was in difficulty, they took money which they held on behalf of the Postmaster-General, intending to repay it at a later stage. In their trial for larceny their defence was twofold: that they lacked intent permanently to deprive as they intended to repay the money; and that, in any event, the taking was not fraudulent. The first part of the defence failed on grounds which were related to the special character of currency. Although they might have intended to reimburse the value of the money which they took, they could not replace the particular coins and notes taken; and it was those coins and notes of which they intended to deprive the Postmaster-General permanently.[3] As to the second part of their defence Lord Goddard agreed with the argument that a meaning must be given to each word in the phrase "fraudulently and without claim of right". The word "fraudulently" means that the taking must be intentional and deliberate and without mistake.[4] The accused were held to have acted fraudulently because they knew that they had no right to take the money which they were aware was not theirs. The intent, or what Lord Goddard called their "hope", to repay was at most a mitigating factor.[5]

28   One point of importance in *Williams* is that the accused, because

98   *R v Holloway* (1849) 2 Car. & K. 942.
99   [1973] Q.B. 530.
1   *Ibid.*, 537.
2   [1953] 1 All E.R. 1068.
3   *Ibid.*, 1070.
4   *Ibid.*
5   *Ibid.*, 1071.

of their financial circumstances, were unlikely to be in a position to repay the money taken. It does not follow that a person who is in such a position would be held to have acted fraudulently in similar circumstances. In a passage which appears in some of the reports of *Williams* Lord Goddard is reported to have said:[6]

> It is one thing if a person with good credit and plenty of money uses somebody else's money which may be in his possession — it having been entrusted to him or he having the opportunity of taking it — he merely intending to use those coins instead of some of his own which he has only to go to his room or to his bank to get. No jury would then say that there was any intent to defraud or any fraudulent taking, but it is quite another matter if the person who takes the money is not in a position to replace it at the time but has only the hope or expectation that he will be able to do so in the future. . . .

Thus, it would appear that the accused's conduct was fraudulent because at the time of the taking they realised that they were not in a position to repay the money. They were fraudulent, therefore, not because they took the money but because, being unable to repay, they realised that they were depriving the owner. But where the accused is in a position to repay at the time it seems that the taking would not be fraudulent. The employee who takes a temporary loan because he is short of cash would not, on this reckoning, be fraudulent.

29   That passage does not appear in the Law Reports or the Criminal Appeal Reports.[7] This discrepancy was crucial in *R v Cockburn*[8] where the accused was charged with the larceny of money which he intended to repay and which he was in a position to do so. The Court of Appeal assumed that Lord Goddard took care to ensure that the quoted passage was removed from the official reports. The Court considered it to be "an extremely dangerous and misleading statement" and presumed that its removal indicated Lord Goddard's concurrence with their view.[9] The accused was held to have acted fraudulently as he took the money without a claim of right. His ability and intention to repay was a matter of mitigation only and did not

6   *Ibid.* 1070; see also [1953] 2 W.L.R. 937, 942.
7   [1953] 1 Q.B. 660; 37 Cr. App. R. 71.
8   [1958] 1 All E.R. 466.
9   *Ibid.*, 468.

negative fraud.[10] The effect of *Cockburn* was to exclude, from English law at least, the defence that the accused's intent and ability to repay negatives fraud. Taken to its logical conclusion *Cockburn* would have strange consequences. An accused who changes a £1 note for two fifty pence coins in his employer's cash register could be guilty of larceny. It was this decision which Lawton LJ had in mind when he suggested that "fraudulently" in the Larceny Act 1916 had acquired a special meaning.[11] As, however, *Cockburn* is not binding in Irish law it is open to the courts to reject it and to interpret fraud in the wide social context which the judgment in *The People (Attorney General) v Grey* would suggest.[12]

---

10 *Ibid.*, 469.
11 *R v Feely* [1973] Q.B. 530.
12 [1944] I.R. 326; see para. 26 *supra*; see however *DPP v Toritelia* [1986] L.R.C. (Crim.) 862.

Section 1

1. For the purposes of this Act —

(1) A person steals who, without the consent of the owner, fraudulently and without a claim of right made in good faith, takes and carries away anything capable of being stolen with intent, at the time of such taking, permanently to deprive the owner thereof:

Provided that a person may be guilty of stealing any such thing notwithstanding that he has lawful possession thereof, if, being a bailee or part owner thereof, he fraudulently converts the same to his own use or the use of any person other than the owner:

(2)—(i) the expression "takes" includes obtaining the possession—

(a) by any trick;

(b) by intimidation;

(c) under a mistake on the part of the owner with knowledge on the part of the taker that possession has been so obtained;

(d) by finding, where at the time of the finding the finder believes that the owner can be discovered by taking reasonable steps;

(ii) the expression "carries away" includes any removal of anything from the place which it occupies, but in the case of a thing attached, only if it has been completely detached;

(iii) the expression "owner" includes any part owner, or person having possession or control of, or a special property in, anything capable of being stolen:

(3) Everything which has value and is the property of any person, and if adhering to the realty then after severance therefrom, shall be capable of being stolen:

Provided that —

(a) save as hereinafter expressly provided with respect to fixtures, growing things, and ore from mines, anything attached to or forming part of the realty shall not be capable of being stolen by the person who severs the same from the realty, unless after severance he has abandoned possession thereof; and

(b) the carcase of a creature wild by nature and not reduced into possession while living shall not be capable of being stolen by the

person who has killed such creature, unless after killing it he has
abandoned possession of the carcase.

30   Section 1, which defines "stealing", can be regarded as the key to the
provisions of the Larceny Act 1916. "Stealing" or "intent to steal"
are ingredients of many of the offences contained in the Act, whilst
the other offences are statutory creations which penalise conduct
which does not amount to "stealing". Thus, section 1 can be viewed
as marking the boundary between larceny and other offences such as
fraudulent conversion, obtaining by false pretences and receiving.
Subsection 1 consists of a codification of larceny at common law,
whilst subsections 2 and 3 elaborate on some of the provisions
contained in subsection 1. In particular, subsection 2 preserves the
various modes of "taking" which amount to larceny, such as larceny
by a trick and larceny by finding, which were developed at common
law, while subsection 3 reiterates the common law principles on
things capable of being stolen. As it is a codifying measure the
pre-existing common law is of especial relevance to the interpretation
of the section. The principal ingredients of the definition will be
considered first, and will be followed by discussion of particular
forms of larceny.

"Without the consent of the owner"

31   The taking of the goods is not larceny if the owner consents to it. The
term "owner" is defined in subsection 2(iii) to include part owners,
persons who have possession or control of goods and those who have
a special property in the goods. In this respect, it should be noted that
an owner can be guilty of the larceny of his own goods, where the
goods are in the possession of a part owner or someone with a special
property in them, such as a bailee.[13] In those circumstances the
relevant consent is that of the limited owner. The taking must be
against the will of the owner and consent may be vitiated by duress,
intimidation or fraud. Where consent is so vitiated the taking amounts
to larceny by intimidation or larceny by a trick.

32   A question might arise as to the owner's consent where he
facilitates the taking in order to trap the accused. A distinction is
drawn between mere facilitation, where the taking is larceny, and a
transfer of the goods, where the taking is not larceny. In *R v Egginton*[14]

13   *Rose v Matt* [1951] 1 All E.R. 361.
14   (1801) 2 Bos. & P. 508.

Definition

an employee was solicited to assist in the stealing of his employer's
goods. On informing the employer he was instructed to continue with
the suggested arrangement and to admit the thieves onto the premises.
The goods, which had been marked, were left in a prominent place
so that the thieves might be apprehended. It was held that the conduct
of the employer did not give rise to a defence. In *R v Turvey*[15] an
employee was urged by the accused to steal goods from his
employer's depot and deliver them to him for sale to a receiver. The
employer instructed the employee to go along with the plan so that
the accused might be apprehended. It was held that the employer, by
his conduct in this instance, consented to the taking. The difference
between the two cases is that in *Egginton* the owner merely made it
easier for the accused to take the goods, whereas in *Turvey* the owner
actually handed the goods over to the accused.

33   The capacity of an employee to consent to the taking of his
employer's goods depends on his authority to deal with them on
behalf of the latter. In *Lacis v Cashmarts*[16] a shopper in a cash-
and-carry store was mistakenly undercharged by the manager. The
shopper was aware of the manager's error and did not bring it to his
attention. It was held that the shopper's knowledge prevented property from passing. However, he was not guilty of larceny as, the
manager having complete authority to deal with his employer's
goods, he took them with the consent of the owner. On the other hand,
if, in similar circumstances, the employee has only a limited authority
to deal with the goods consent of the owner is absent.[17]

"Fraudulently and without claim of right made in good faith"
34   The concept of fraud has been discussed earlier[18] and it has been noted
that fraud is the outstanding characteristic of larceny.[19] Although the
courts have been reluctant to provide an exhaustive definition of
fraud, it has been remarked that it involves dishonest or immoral
conduct on the part of the accused.[20] It has been suggested that, despite

15 [1946] 2 All E.R. 60.
16 [1969] 2 Q.B. 440; see also *R v Prince* (1868) L.R. 1 C.C.R. 150.
17 See *R v Middleton* (1873) L.R. 2 C.C.R. 38.
18 See paras. 23-29 *supra*.
19 *The People (Attorney General) v Grey* [1944] I.R. 326, 331.
20 *Ibid.*, 332.

24

English authority to the contrary,[21] fraud should be tested in the light of prevailing social standards of dishonesty and should not be equated solely with the absence of a claim of right.[22] In practice, however, the accused is likely to attempt to negative fraud by asserting a claim of right. The claim of right must be in good faith, that is, the accused must genuinely have believed that his conduct was justified. It is well established that a claim of right need not be founded on a right recognised by law; it is sufficient that the accused honestly believed that he was entitled to take the goods. In *R v Bernhard*[23] the accused's belief that she was entitled to enforce what, in fact, was an unenforceable contract was a defence to demanding with menaces with intent to steal. That decision was endorsed by the Court of Criminal Appeal in *The People (Attorney General) v Grey*.[24] The accused, a company secretary whose contract of employment entitled him to free gas and fuel, was charged with the fraudulent conversion of batteries which belonged to the company. Due to the prevailing war conditions the company was unable to provide him with free fuel, and he took the batteries in what he believed to be lawful substitution of his contractual entitlement. The Court held the defence of claim of right to have been successfully raised. In *The People (DPP) v O'Loughlin*[25] the accused's belief that he was entitled to take goods in order to enforce the payment of a debt which was due to him was held to constitute a claim of right.

"Takes"

35   The expression "takes" is expanded in subsection 2(i) and includes taking by a trick, by intimidation, by mistake and by finding. Consideration of those forms of taking has been deferred.[26] In essence, taking involves a trespassory interference by the accused with the possession of the goods in question. It must be established that the accused removed the goods from the possession of the prosecutor. This point is crucial, since if possession by the prosecutor can not be established, or if the accused acquired possession innocently, there is no larceny. Possession has developed into an

---

21 *R v Cockburn* [1958] 1 All E.R. 466; see also *R v Feely* [1973] Q.B. 530.
22 See para. 26, *supra*.
23 [1938] 2 K.B. 164.
24 [1944] I.R. 326.
25 [1979] I.R. 85.
26 See paras 49-53 *infra*..

intricate set of rules, many of which are peculiar to the law of larceny. The concept of possession has been considered earlier and it is not proposed to repeat that discussion.[27] It is sufficient to note that, whilst in most cases goods will be in both the physical custody and possession of the same person, custody does not necessarily involve possession. Goods which are in the custody of one person can be in the possession of another. If, in those circumstances, the custodian converts the goods he removes them from the possession of the owner. Possession implies control over the goods and the person with the right to exercise that control is the possessor.[28] In addition, possession requires knowledge by the supposed possessor of the existence of the thing alleged to be possessed.[29] Consequently, a person who is unaware of its existence is considered not to possess it. However, that general proposition is qualified by the rule that a landowner acquires constructive possession of articles which are abandoned on his land, since the landowner would not necessarily have the required knowledge.[30] The rule was explained by Lord Goddard in *Hibbert v McKiernan*[31] on the basis that every landowner means or intends to exclude wrongdoers from his land and that confers a special property in goods found on his land. It should be noted that in that case the landowner took active steps to exclude wrongdoers and Humphries and Pritchard JJ emphasised that factor. However, regardless of its underlying explanation the rule is well established and operates as an exception to the general rule which requires knowledge. It would appear that knowledge of the existence of the goods is sufficient and that knowledge as to their quality is not required. This point will be considered later.[32]

36   Goods remain in the possession of the prosecutor who delivers them to the accused where the delivery is for what is variously termed a temporary, special or limited purpose. The delivery for that purpose implies that the prosecutor retains the right to demand the return of the goods or otherwise to dispose of them. Consequently, the accused, in those circumstances, merely has custody, not possession. If the

27 See paras 13-22, *supra.*
28 *Minister for Posts and Telegraphs v Campbell* [1966] I.R. 69; *The People (Attorney General) v Nugent and Byrne* (1964) 98 I.L.T.R. 139, 1 Frewen 294.
29 *Ibid.*
30 *R v Rowe* (1859) Bell C.C. 93; *R v Foley* (1889) 26 L.R. Ir. 299.
31 [1948] 2 K.B. 142.
32 See para. 52 *infra.*

accused absconds with the goods that constitutes a taking and, all other things being equal, amounts to larceny. Examples of possession remaining in the prosecutor include: handing over of goods by a shopkeeper to a prospective purchaser for examination;[33] giving money to someone who is at the head of a queue to purchase a ticket;[34] entrusting a person with the delivery of goods to a particular destination;[35] delivery of goods by an employer to an employee in the course of the employment.[36] Likewise, gas contained in pipes belonging to the accused is in the possession of the gas company until it passes through the meter.[37] These decisions can be explained by the presumed intent of the prosecutor not to yield control over the goods. In *O'Toole v Samuels*[38] the accused, who found stolen money in his garden, kept it until it could be identified. On learning of this, the owner asked him to retain the money until it could be collected. The accused subsequently refused to surrender the money to the owner. That was held to amount to a taking as the owner intended the accused to have physical custody and did not part with possession of the money. In *DPP v Morrissey*[39] the accused, who was given meat at the meat-counter of a supermarket, concealed it and left without paying. It was held that the meat was given to the accused on condition that he pay the cashier for it. Accordingly, the accused merely had custody of the meat and the owner retained a continuing right to determine that custody. Gannon J did not expressly refer to the owner's intent, but did state that the only inference to be drawn was that the accused was required to pay for the meat and acquired it with that knowledge.[40] In contrast, if the accused delivers goods to the prosecutor for a temporary purpose the latter does not acquire

33 *R v Chisser* (1678) T. Raym. 275.
34 *R v Thompson* (1862) Le. & Ca. 225; see *contra R v Thomas* (1841) 9 Car. & P. 741.
35 *R v Colhoun* (1842) 2 Cr. & D. 57. But see *R v Brennan* (1840) 1 Cr. & D. 560 where the accused, who was given money by the prosecutor to hold for him, was found not to be guilty when she refused to return them as she lacked intent at the time of delivery. Her conduct was deemed to be no more than a breach of trust. It is submitted that she would now be found guilty either of larceny as a bailee or, possibly, of fraudulent conversion under s. 20.
36 Coke, *Third Inst.* 108 (1506); *R v Bass* (1782) 1 Leach 251.
37 *R v White* (1853) Dears. 203.
38 (1972) 3 S.A.S.R. 30.
39 [1982] I.L.R.M. 487.
40 *Ibid.*, 490; see also *Martin v Puttick* [1968] 1 Q.B. 82.

sufficient possession to support a conviction for larceny. Thus, where the accused handed the prosecutor a blank receipt, and informed him that he would pay a debt which was due, it was not a taking when the accused absconded with the signed receipt without paying.[41]

37 Where goods are delivered by a third party to the accused on behalf of the prosecutor they do not immediately fall into the latter's possession. Although the prosecutor might have acquired possession for the purposes of civil law,[42] or in respect of third persons,[43] with respect to the accused something more must happen before the goods are deemed to be in his possession. Instead, they are considered to be in the exclusive possession of the accused and if the accused misappropriates the goods immediately on delivery it is not larceny. Thus, an employee who converts money paid by a customer, before the money is placed in the cash register, is not guilty of larceny.[44] However, once the accused does an act which determines his exclusive possession the goods come into the constructive possession of the prosecutor.[45] For instance, the placing of money in a cash register or the putting of goods in the employer's truck or warehouse establishes his constructive possession,[46] and a subsequent misappropriation amounts to a taking.

38 To constitute larceny the taking must amount to a trespass.[47] This requirement was based on the view that if the prosecutor could not maintain an action in trespass against the accused he lacked sufficient possession for the purposes of larceny.[48] If, in this respect, the initial taking is innocent a subsequent conversion of the goods is not larceny. In *R v Davies*[49] the accused acquired a car which he later learned to have been stolen. His refusal to return the car to the owner was held not to amount to larceny as his original taking was not a trespass. Conversely, there is English authority to the effect that if the initial

41 *R v Frampton* (1846) 2 Car. & K. 50; *R v Smith* (1852) 2 Den. 449.

42 *R v Waite* (1743) 1 Leach 28.

43 *R v Reed* (1854) Dears 168, 257.

44 *R v Bazeley* (1799) 2 Leach 835.

45 *R v Reed* (1854) Dears 168, 257.

46 But see *R v Abrahat* (1798) 2 Leach 824, *R v Spears* (1798) 2 Leach 825. In *Williams v Phillips* (1957) 41 Cr. App. R. 5, it was held that refuse placed in dustbins for collection passes into the constructive possession of the local authority; binmen who took items from the bins were guilty of larceny.

47 See Turner, "Larceny and Trespass" (1942) 58 L.Q.R. 340.

48 *R v Smith* (1852) 2 Den. 449.

49 [1970] V.R. 27.

taking amounts to a trespass a subsequent conversion of the goods can complete the larceny. In *R v Riley*[50] the accused removed his sheep from the prosecutor's field. He was unaware, at the time, that one of the prosecutor's sheep had joined his flock. When he noticed the additional sheep, which he knew not to be his, he sold it and kept the proceeds. He was convicted of larceny, the court being satisfied that the initial taking was trespassory, not innocent.[51] It has earlier been submitted that *Riley* ought not to be followed in this jurisdiction as the taking should have been considered to be innocent.[52] It has also been suggested that an initial trespass is not sufficient to make the conversion larcenous where the taking was not accompanied by fraudulent intent.[53]

39   It is not essential that the accused was the person who performed the taking. A taking can be achieved through the use of an innocent agent, such as an infant who is below the age of discretion or a person who is innocent of intent but whose participation was fraudulently procured by the accused.[54] In *R v Pitman*[55] the accused directed an ostler to bring him a horse which he intended to steal. The horse became agitated as the accused attempted to mount and he directed the ostler to take it out of the yard. He was apprehended before he could renew his efforts to mount the horse. It was held that there was a sufficient taking as the accused had caused the animal to be removed for his "accommodation and procurement".

"Carries away"

40 This ingredient, which is expanded in subsection 2(ii), is what at common law was termed "asportation". In short, the accused must have moved the goods, however slightly, from their original location. Thus, simply to place one's hands on the goods with a view to removing them is not sufficient. Usually the carrying away will be self evident in the taking, but they are separate ingredients and the former has been the subject of several decisions. In *R v Taylor*[56] the

50 (1853) Dears. 149.
51 See also *Ruse v Read* [1949] 1 All E.R. 398; *Minigall v McCammon* [1970] S.A.S.R. 82.
52 See para. 17 *supra*.
53 *Ibid*.
54 2 East P.C. 555; see *R v Wallis* (1848) 3 Cox C.C. 67.
55 (1826) 2 Car. & P. 423.
56 [1911] 1 K.B. 674.

accused put his hand in the prosecutor's pocket and removed the latter's purse. The purse, however, was caught in the prosecutor's belt and the accused was apprehended. It was held that there was not a sufficient asportation to support a conviction of larceny from the person.[57] However, the accused was guilty of simple larceny as the purse had been moved from its original position at the bottom of the pocket to the edge of the belt. In *Wallis v Lane*[58] the accused who, with intent to steal, moved goods from one part of a truck to another was held to be guilty of larceny, there being a sufficient asportation.[59] Where the goods are attached to something asportation is complete only when they are severed; it is not sufficient to move them only as far as the rope or chain by which they are attached allows.[60]

"Anything capable of being stolen"

41 This expression, which is expanded in subsection 3, codifies the common law rules on what is the subject of larceny. Briefly stated, the thing must be tangible, moveable, of value and the property of somebody. Real property and choses in action are not capable of being stolen. Thus, the sale of pirated music does not amount to larceny, as all the prosecutor is deprived of is the intangible right of copyright.[61] Occasionally a question might arise as to whether the thing taken is tangible or not. This is principally a question of fact and can presumably be determined with the aid of expert testimony, where necessary. Gas which is supplied by a gas company is capable of being stolen,[62] as is water which is supplied by a water company.[63] It would

57 See also *The People (Attorney General) v Mills* (1955) 1 Frewen 153.

58 [1964] V.R. 293.

59 See also *R v Cozlett* (1782) 2 East P.C. 556; *State v Carswell* (1978) 296 N.C. 101, 249 S.E. 2d 427.

60 *R v Wilkinson* (1598) 2 East P.C. 556; *Anon.* (1781) 2 East P.C. 556.

61 *R v Kidd* (1907) 72 J.P. 104. The person who wrongfully appropriates intangible property could indirectly be convicted by charging him with the larceny of the thing (*e.g.* paper or cassette) on which the matter is recorded, assuming that he also took that thing from the owner's possession; see *R v Perry* (1845) 1 Car. & K. 726. In *Oxford v Moss* (1978) 68 Cr. App. R. 183 it was held that confidential information is not "property" for the purposes of s. 4(1) of the English Theft Act 1968. As "property" is defined more widely than "anything capable of being stolen" the position would be the same under the Larceny Act 1916.

62 *R v White* (1853) Dears. 203. It can be presumed that gas stored in a container is capable of being stolen.

63 *Ferens v O'Brien* (1883) 11 Q.B.D. 21. However, water in its natural condition is not, it would seem, capable of being stolen.

appear that, given its nature, electricity is not capable of being stolen;[64] however, the fraudulent abstraction of electricity is an offence under section 10.

42   It is now settled that the thing need not have an assignable value; in other words, it need not have the value of a known coin.[65] Thus, something which would be considered to be virtually worthless can, nonetheless, be stolen as presumably it would have some notional value. For example, the taking of a void cheque amounts to larceny of a piece of paper,[66] as does the taking of a copy which was made of a subsequently discarded document.[67] For practical purposes, therefore, the requirement that the thing be of value is unimportant. Things in which the law does not recognise any property are not capable of being stolen.[68] These include abandoned articles, wild animals,[69] seaweed which lies ungathered between the high and low water marks[70] and dead bodies.[71] Coffins and winding sheets in which corpses are placed are the subject of larceny, as property remains in those who owned them at the time of burial.[72] However, abandoned articles and wild animals become larcenable when reduced into

64 *Low v Blease* [1975] Crim. L.R. 513.

65 *R v Morris* (1840) 9 Car. & P. 349.

66 *R v Perry* (1845) 1 Car. & K. 726.

67 *R v A.B.* [1941] 1 K.B. 454.

68 In *R v Smith* (1819) 1 Cr. & D.155 it was held that property in money collected in a charity plate at church vests immediately in the treasurer. Thus, the contributor who changes his mind and withdraws his contribution would be guilty of larceny. But in *R v Thompson* (1862) Le. & Ca. 225, 228 Williams J referred to a case tried before Maule J where the collector of sacrament money was found guilty of the larceny of a coin which was put on the plate on a count which laid property in the contributor.

69 See *R v Howlett* [1968] Crim. L.R. 222 where it was conceded that mussels found on the seashore are animals wild by nature. It should be noted that the taking of certain animals is an offence under the Larceny Act 1861; birds or beasts ordinarily kept in confinement (s. 21), house doves or house pigeons (s. 23) and fish in water on private property or in which there is a private right of fishing (s. 24).

70 *R v Clinton* (1869) I.R. 4 C.L. 6.

71 *R v Haynes* (1614) 12 Co. Rep. 113; *R v Sharpe* (1857) Dears. & Bell 160. It is a common law misdemeanour to remove a corpse from a burial ground. This exclusion from larceny seems to be based on the proposition that there is no property in a corpse. But it is possible that specimens from a living body, or organs preserved for transplanting are the subject of larceny; see Griew, *The Theft Acts 1968 and 1978* (London, 1986) paras. 2-18 — 2-20.

72 *R v Haynes* (1614) 12 Co. Rep. 113.

possession. They will either be in the actual possession of the person who acquired them or in the constructive possession of the landowner on whose land they are left.[73] Similarly, sea fish are the subject of larceny once they have been landed, as they have come into the possession of the trawler owner.[74] In *R v Townley*[75] a poacher killed rabbits on land owned by the Crown. He placed the dead rabbits in various places on the land, intending to collect them at the end of the hunt. It was held that his conduct amounted to a continuous transaction, that the rabbits remained in his actual possession and, accordingly, did not come into the constructive possession of the landowner.

43   The rule that real property is not capable of being stolen was extended to include things attached to the realty and things which savour of the realty, such as title deeds. Things attached to the land include both thing growing on the land and fixtures. In considering whether a thing is a fixture the court will have regard to the object of annexation.[76] The larceny of wills and documents of title is an offence under sections 6 and 7 respectively. The larceny of ore from mines is an offence under section 11. On the other hand, things attached to the land are not capable of being stolen unless, having been removed, they have been abandoned and revert to the constructive possession of the landowner. In *R v Foley*[77] the accused cut grass which was growing on the prosecutor's land, left it lying on the land and returned three days later to gather and remove it. It was held that the accused, by leaving the grass on the ground, ceased to have actual possession and that it fell into the constructive possession of the landowner. By removing it he took it from the landowner's possession and was guilty of larceny. The Court endorsed the concept of continuous transaction which was central to *R v Townley*,[78] but held that continuity was broken by the accused's leaving the grass uncollected for three days. It is not readily apparent in *Foley* why continuity was broken. The majority held that the accused's intention not to abandon was

---

73   *R v Foley* (1889) 26 L.R. Ir. 299; *Hibbert v McKiernan* [1948] 1 All E.R. 860; *R v Shickle* (1868) L.R. 1 C.C.R. 158.

74   *R v Mallinson* (1902) 20 Cox C.C. 204.

75   (1871) L.R. 1 C.C.R. 315.

76   *Billing v Pill* [1953] 2 All E.R. 1061; *R v Skujins* [1956] Crim. L.R. 266; see Wylie, *Irish Land Law* (Abingdon, 1986) pp. 167, 819, 821. The stealing or damaging of fixtures and trees with intent to steal is an offence under s. 8.

77   (1889) 26 L.R. Ir. 299.

78   (1871) L.R. 1 C.C.R. 315.

immaterial; the question was whether he was in continuous actual, though not necessarily physical, possession. Possibly the length of time which elapsed between the cutting and gathering of the grass influenced the Court, but this was not expressed in the judgments. In *Townley* the killing and collection of the rabbits was considered to be part of a continuous transaction, namely the hunt in which the accused was engaged. But could not the cutting and later gathering of grass be the continuous transaction of collecting hay?

44   In *R v Edwards and Stacey*[79] the accused were charged with the larceny of three diseased pigs which the prosecutor had shot and buried. In their defence it was argued that the pigs were not the subject of larceny as they had been abandoned, that they were of no value to the prosecutor and that they formed part of the realty. Those contentions were rejected as being unfounded. With respect to abandonment the Court directed that there had been no abandonment as the prosecutor had intended to prevent further use being made of them.

"With intent, at the time of such taking, permanently to deprive the owner thereof"

45   It is essential that the intent coincides with the taking, that is with the acquisition of possession. Thus, the accused is not guilty of larceny if the taking was innocent, regardless of his subsequent state of mind. In *R v Leigh*[80] the accused, who saved goods from the prosecutor's burning shop, subsequently misappropriated them. She was held not to be guilty of larceny as the original taking was not done with intent to steal. The necessary coincidence of intent and taking has led to the development of rules which postponed the taking until the accused formed intent.[81] The principal devices adopted were the rule which emerged from *R v Riley*,[82] that if the taking was trespassory the later formation of intent completed the offence, and the rule to the effect that the accused does not acquire possession unless he has knowledge of the goods.[83] Despite confusion in the authorities certain observations can be made. If at the time the goods are delivered to him the accused is aware of a mistake on the part of the owner the

79   (1877) 13 Cox C.C. 384.
80   (1800) 2 East P.C. 694.
81   See paras 13-22 *supra*.
82   (1853) Dears. 149.
83   See paras 14 and 18-22 *supra*.

offence is complete.[84] On the other hand, the conclusion from *R v Hehir*[85] is that if, at the time of delivery, the accused knows of the existence of the goods, but is ignorant as to some quality of the goods, possession passes and the accused's later formation of intent, on learning of that quality, is immaterial. The crucial distinction made in *Hehir* is between knowledge of the existence of the goods and knowledge of their qualities. Knowledge of the first type is sufficient to pass possession. Thus, where the prosecutor pays to the accused a sum which the accused is aware is greater than the prosecutor believes it to be larceny is committed. But, where the prosecutor pays the accused a sum which is greater than that which both parties believe it to be no offence is committed, even though the accused converts the additional money on discovering the error; the error is merely one as to a quality of the goods. If, however, the accused is unaware of the existence of the goods possession will not pass. Where an accused is not aware of the existence of the contents of a container which is in his possession he would probably be considered not to possess those contents.[86] Accordingly, if on learning of their existence the accused decides to appropriate the contents larceny is committed. It is submitted that the English decisions to the effect that the accused acquires possession only if the deliverer intends, albeit mistakenly, to give him the goods are inconsistent with *Hehir* and should not be adopted.[87] Those decisions were based on the judgments which favoured upholding the conviction in *R v Ashwell*,[88] and which were rejected in *Hehir*. It is further submitted that the doctrine of continuing trespass which derives from *R v Riley* should not be adopted in this jurisdiction. If the accused lacks intent at the time he acquires possession, albeit unlawful, his later formation of intent should not matter.[89]

46   The intent required is to deprive the owner permanently of the goods or, in the case of an owner charged with the larceny of his own goods, to deprive the special owner of his rights in respect of the

---

84   *R v Middleton* (1873) L.R. 2 C.C.R. 38.

85   [1895] 2 I.R. 709.

86   *Warner v Metropolitan Police Commissioner* [1969] 2 A.C. 256; see *contra Minigall v McCammon* [1970] S.A.S.R. 82, 91.

87   *R v Hudson* [1943] 1 All E.R. 642; *Russell v Smith* [1957] 2 All E.R. 796; see paras 20-21 *supra*.

88   (1885) 16 Q.B.D. 190.

89   See para. 17 *supra*.

goods.[90] Where the accused's intention falls short of one to deprive permanently the taking is not larceny. Thus, if the taker merely "borrows" the goods, or otherwise intends eventually to return them to the owner, no larceny is committed. In *R v Phillips and Strong*[91] the accused took two horses and left them at an inn some distance from the owner's premises. On the jury's finding that they only wanted to ride the horses and did not intend to make any further use of them, it was held that they lacked intent.[92] Equally, it would appear that a "conditional" intent does not suffice. Thus, if the accused, at the time of taking, has it in mind to deprive the owner of the goods only if they prove to be worth taking he lacks the necessary intent.[93] In most cases the intent will be established on proof of the accused's having converted the goods to his own use or having benefitted from their disposal. It should be noted that personal enrichment is not necessary as long as the intent is to deprive the owner permanently. The destruction of the goods amounts to a permanent deprivation and an intent to destroy them suffices.[94]

Larceny by a bailee or part owner

47 Unless he "broke bulk",[95] a bailee, at common law, could not commit larceny as his possession of the goods was lawful. The proviso in subsection 1, which re-enacts earlier statutory provisions,[96] allows for the conviction of a bailee or part owner who fraudulently converts goods to his own use or to that of a third party. The essence of the offence is that the bailee forms the intent to deprive the owner after he has acquired possession. The accused must be under an obligation to return the goods to the owner or to deliver them to a third party. Usually the obligation will be contractual, but this is not an essential requirement. In *R v McDonald*[97] the accused sold to a third party goods which he had hired. Although the contract was void due to the accused's infancy, it was held that he was a bailee. It was stated that bailment is complete on delivery of goods on trust or condition which

---

90 *Rose v Matt* [1951] 1 All E.R. 361; *R v Wilkinson and Marsden* (1821) Russ. & Ry. 470.
91 (1801) 2 East P.C. 662.
92 See also *R v Crump* (1825) 1 Car. & P. 658.
93 *R v Easom* [1971] 2 Q.B. 315.
94 *R v Jones* (1846) 2 Car. & K. 114; *R v Wynn* (1849) 2 Car. & K. 859.
95 See para. 5 *supra*.
96 Prevention of Frauds Act 1857, s. 4; Larceny Act 1861, s. 3.
97 (1885) 15 Q.B.D. 323.

creates a special property in the accused. In *R v Clegg*[98] the accused's father contracted to save the cargo of a wrecked ship. The accused took possession of the ship and saved part of the cargo, which he later sold, keeping the proceeds. A majority of the Court for Crown Cases Reserved held that there was sufficient evidence to conclude that the accused was a bailee.

48   To be guilty of the offence it must be established that the bailee fraudulently converted the goods. Normally this will be established by proof that he sold or otherwise disposed of them to his or a third party's benefit. However, it is not essential that the bailee profited or that the owner suffered a loss. In general, conversion consists of conduct by which the bailee asserts full title to the goods adverse to that of the owner. In *Rogers v Arnott*[99] the accused, who offered goods for sale contrary to the terms of the bailment under which they were held, was convicted of larceny. That act was sufficient to evince his intention to deprive the owner of his rights in respect of the goods. A point of comparative interest is that fraudulent conversion, under section 20, may be established circumstantially by proof that the accused was under a duty to account for the property or to deliver it and failed to do so.[1] However, it should be noted that larceny and fraudulent conversion are discrete offences.[2]

Larceny by a trick

49   This is not a separate species of larceny but is a method of "taking" which has been termed "constructive" taking.[3] It occurs where the prosecutor was induced by some trick to deliver the goods to the accused. The trick need not be disclosed to the prosecutor and an uncommunicated intention to deprive suffices. In this respect tricks differ from false pretences.[4] It is essential that the accused had intent at the time of the delivery.[5] The accused's fraudulent intent precludes possession from passing at that time and the wrongful acquisition of possession occurs on the accused's subsequent conversion of the

---

98   (1869) I.R. 3 C.L. 166.
99   [1960] 2 All E.R. 418.
1   *The People (Attorney General) v Murphy* (1947) 1 Frewen 85.
2   See para. 80 *infra*.
3   *R v Rogers* (1841) 1 Cases on the Six Circuits 280.
4   As to false pretences see paras 143-151 *infra*.
5   *R v Rogers* (1841) 1 Cases on the Six Circuits 280; *R v Banks* (1821) Russ. & Ry. 441.

goods.[6] Larceny by a trick is committed where the prosecutor intended to part with possession of, but not property in, the goods.[7] Thus, an accused who induces a prosecutor to part with goods on a bailment and who later converts them is guilty,[8] as is an accused who induces the prosecutor to part with goods on cash, but not credit, terms.[9] Where, however, the prosecutor intends to part with both possession of and property in the goods the offence, if any, is obtaining by false pretences.[10] Expressed in civil law terms the difference between the two offences corresponds to that between the delivery of goods under a void contract, which is larceny by a trick, and delivery under a voidable contract, which is obtaining by false pretences.[11]

50   The distinction between the two offences is not always clear in practice. In *R v Russett*[12] the prosecutor and accused agreed to the sale of a horse on which a deposit was to be paid immediately and the balance on delivery. The accused never intended to complete the sale and was found guilty of larceny by a trick. The court considered that by paying a deposit the prosecutor did not intend to part with property in the money.[13] That conclusion is questionable, especially in view of the prosecutor's testimony that he expected not to see the money but to have the horse, which would suggest that, in fact, he intended to part with property in the money. In this respect, the conclusion reached is difficult to support. *Russett* was distinguished in *R v Collins*[14] where the accused, who was paid the purchase price in advance, was held to be not guilty of larceny. The money paid in the earlier case was a recoverable deposit and, thus, it would not be envisaged that property would pass until the goods were delivered, whereas property in an advance payment would be intended to pass immediately. More problematic is the suggestion in *R v Jones*[15] where the accused was given an advance payment to purchase materials for

6   *R v Pear* (1779) 1 Leach 212.
7   *R v Aikles* (1784) 1 Leach 294; *R v Russett* [1892] 2 Q.B. 312.
8   *R v Pear* (1779) 1 Leach 212.
9   *R v Slowly and Humphrey* (1873) 12 Cox C.C. 269.
10 *R v Parkes* (1794) 2 Leach 614; see also *Anderson v Ryan* [1967] I.R. 64.
11 See *Whitehorn Bros. v Davison* [1911] 1 K.B. 463; *Pearson v Rose and Young* [1951] 1 K.B. 275.
12 [1892] 2 Q.B. 312.
13 See also *R v Stephens* (1910) 4 Cr. App. R. 52.
14 (1922) 17 Cr. App. R. 42.
15 (1948) 33 Cr. App. R. 11.

decorating work which he undertook to do. His conviction of fraudulent conversion was quashed and Lord Goddard, equating the case with that of a welshing bookmaker,[16] expressed the opinion that he could have been convicted of larceny by a trick. However, the welshing bookmaker is guilty of larceny by a trick because the owner does not intend to part with property in the money. But can it be said that someone who gives a decorator money to purchase paint intends to retain property in that money?

Larceny by intimidation

51 Where threats or duress are used to secure the delivery of goods it is clear that the owner's consent has been vitiated. Moreover, delivery induced by intimidation constitutes a taking. In *R v McGrath*[17] the prosecutrix attended a mock auction at which the accused alleged that she bid for a particular item. When she denied this and refused to pay she was told that she would not be allowed to leave until she paid the sum requested. She paid under protest and the accused was held to be guilty of larceny by intimidation. Many cases of larceny by intimidation would now probably also amount to robbery, which requires the use, or threatened use, of force.[18]

Larceny by mistake

52 Where the owner mistakenly delivers goods to the accused who at the time is aware of the mistake it is larceny. This, in effect, is a statutory expression of the decision in *R v Middleton*.[19] There the accused, a post-office depositor, wished to withdraw a sum from his account and presented his deposit book to this end. By mistake the clerk placed a larger sum on the counter and the accused, noticing this, picked up the money and left. He was held guilty of larceny. That decision is confined to cases where the accused is aware of the mistake at the time he takes delivery of the goods. If, on the other hand, the accused is unaware that he has been overpaid the taking does not amount to larceny even though he decides, on discovering the error, to convert the excess payment.[20] It would appear that the accused is guilty only

16 *R v Buckmaster* (1887) 20 Q.B.D. 182.
17 (1869) L.R. 1 C.C.R. 205; see also Hooper, "Larceny by Intimidation - 1" [1965] Crim. L.R. 532.
18 See paras 92-96 *infra*.
19 (1873) L.R. 2 C.C.R. 38.
20 *R v Hehir* [1895] 2 I.R. 709.

where he is mistaken as to the existence of the goods, or, possibly, believes them to be something different from that which they are, and decides to convert them on discovering their identity. Thus, an accused who is handed what is believed to be an empty envelope but which, in fact, contains money would be guilty if on discovering the money he decides to convert it. The same result might follow where the accused believes the goods to be radically different from that which they are such as believing a currency note to be a lottery ticket.[21]

Larceny by finding

53 A finder is guilty of larceny where at the time of finding he is aware of the identity of the owner or believes that the owner can be traced by the making of reasonable efforts on his part. The crucial factor is the accused's state of mind at the time of the finding.[22] If, at that time, the accused believes that the goods were abandoned, or that the owner's identity cannot be discovered with reasonable efforts on his part, he acquires lawful possession, which is subject only to the owner's superior right.[23] Consequently, a subsequent discovery that the goods were not abandoned, or of the owner's identity, does not make the conversion larcenous.[24] What constitutes reasonable efforts will depend on the facts of the case, in particular the place where the goods were found, their nature and any identifying marks which might accompany them. The existence of a facility for the deposit of lost goods, such as a lost-and-found office, would be relevant to the question whether the owner could have been found with reasonable efforts. Likewise, the finding of goods in a place to which it could be

---

21 See paras 18-21 *supra*.

22 *R v Breen* (1843) 3 Cr. & D. 30; *R v Deaves* (1869) I.R. 3 C.L. 306; *R v Thurborn* (1849) 1 Den 387; see also *R v McGowan* (1824) 1 Cr. & D. 161; *Anon* (1831) 1 Cr. & D. 161.

23 In *Minigall v McCammon* [1970] S.A.S.R. 82, 84-87 Bray CJ suggested that only where he picks up the goods in the hope of being able to return them to the owner does a finder acquire lawful possession, on the basis of the owner's implied consent. On the other hand, if the finder believes the goods to be abandoned or the owner not to be discoverable his acquisition of possession is trespassory, but he is not guilty by reason of his initial innocent intention. But if the finder has no belief or intent with respect to the goods the taking is a trespass and, applying *R v Riley* (1853) Dears. 149, a later conversion of the goods is larceny.

24 *R v Breen* (1843) 3 Cr. & D. 30; *R v Deaves* (1869) I.R. 3 C.L. 306.

expected that the owner would return would be relevant.[25] Equally, if the goods were particularly valuable it could be assumed that the owner could be traced by taking such steps as consulting the police, to whom it might be expected the owner would report his loss, or by having recourse to lost-and-found advertisments.

Evidence of recent possession[26]

54 In some cases the prosecution will seek to rely on evidence that the accused was found in possession of goods or housebreaking implements shortly after the theft, in support of a charge of larceny. Whilst such evidence is admissible,[27] it does not place an onus on the accused to establish that the possession was innocent and it is misdirection to suggest otherwise.[28] However, inferences of guilt might reasonably be drawn if the accused fails to explain his possession.[29] Recent possession can be evidence either of larceny or of receiving and it is for the jury to determine which offence, if any, has been committed.[30] Where the possession is so close to the theft as to exclude the possibility of anyone other than the accused having had possession the larceny charge only should go to the jury.[31] Moreover, recent possession is also evidence of any aggravating circumstances, such as threats or menaces, which might have accompanied the larceny.[32]

---

25 *R v Moore* (1861) 3 Le. & Ca. 1 — a shopkeeper who found money in his shop was held guilty of larceny as it could be assumed that the money was lost by one of his customers.

26 See paras 156-158 *infra.*

27 See *The People (Attorney General) v Sykes* [1958] I.R. 355.

28 *The People (Attorney General) v Oglesby* [1966] I.R. 163.

29 *Ibid.*

30 *R v McMahon* (1875) 13 Cox C.C. 275; *The People (Attorney General) v Finnigan* [1933] I.R. 292.

31 *The People (Attorney General) v Carney and Mulcahy* [1955] I.R. 324.

32 *R v Atkinson* (1825) 1 Cr. & D. 161; *R v Stapleton* (1841) 2 Cr. & D. 87. In *Atkinson* it was remarked that the finding of a banknote in the accused's possession is of slight evidential value.

Section 2

[SIMPLE LARCENY]

2. Stealing for which no special punishment is provided under this or any other Act for the time being in force shall be simple larceny and a felony punishable with penal servitude for any term not exceeding five years, and the offender, if a male under the age of sixteen years, shall be liable to be once privately whipped in addition to any other punishment to which he may by law be liable.

55 In *The State (Foley) v Carroll*[33] it was held that the section merely provides a penalty for the common law offence of larceny. The inclusion in an indictment of the words "contrary to section 2" does not render it bad, such words being surplusage.[34] Where the prosecution chooses to charge the accused with simple larceny, rather than with an aggravated form of larceny of which he might be guilty, it is not a defence to show that there were circumstances of aggravation.[35] In such a case a prosecution under this section merely limits the penalty which may be imposed. The decision in *The State (Foley) v Carroll* can be contrasted with the earlier decision of the Court of Criminal Appeal in *The People (Attorney General) v Mills*.[36] In the latter case it was held that an accused, whose conduct amounted to a larceny from the person, contrary to section 14, should not have been convicted under section 2, the Court being of the view that simple larceny and larceny from the person were discrete offences. *Mills* was not referred to in *The State (Foley) v Carroll*, but it is submitted that, on principle, the later decision is preferable.

---

33 [1980] I.R. 150.

34 *The State (Simmonds) v Governor of Portlaoise Prison* Supreme Court, June 25, 1968 (ex tempore) — noted [1980] I.R. 150, 151.

35 [1980] I.R. 150, 154; see also *R v Blackburne* (1841) 2 Cr & D 188.

36 (1955) 1 Frewen 153.

Section 3

[LARCENY OF CATTLE]

3. Every person who steals any horse, cattle, or sheep shall be guilty of felony, and on conviction thereof liable to penal servitude for any term not exceeding fourteen years.

56 Section 3, which provides an aggravated punishment, applies to the larceny of live animals and the stealing of dead animals must be prosecuted as simple larceny.[37]

Section 4

[KILLING ANIMALS WITH INTENT TO STEAL]

4. Every person who wilfully kills any animal with intent to steal the carcase skin, or any part of the animal killed, shall be guilty of felony, and on conviction thereof liable to the same punishment as if he had stolen such animal, provided that the offence of stealing the animal so killed would have amounted to felony.

57 It is sufficient for the purposes of this section that the accused killed the animal with intent to steal and proof of stealing is not necessary. With regard to the intent required reference must be made to the definition of stealing in section 1. Thus, a claim of right would be a defence.[38] It would appear that the administering of a fatal wound to the animal amounts to killing and, if done with intent to steal, is an offence under the section. In *R v Clay*[39] the accused cut a leg from a live lamb which died shortly afterwards from the wound. It was held that by giving a deadly wound the accused killed with intent to steal. Whether the animal dies from the wound administered by the accused

37 *R v Williams* (1825) 1 Mood. 107.
38 See *R v Bernhard* [1938] 2 K.B. 164; *The People (Attorney General) v Grey* [1944] I.R. 326.
39 (1819) R. & R. 387.

is a question of causation and the fact that unsuccessful attempts made to save the animal prolong its life is immaterial.[40] Where the accused kills an animal and removes portion of its carcase he may also be convicted of larceny.[41]

Section 5
[LARCENY, &c., OF DOGS]

5. Every person who —

(1) steals any dog after a previous summary conviction of any such offence; or

(2) unlawfully has in his possession or on his premises any stolen dog, or the skin thereof, knowing such dog or skin to have been stolen, after a previous summary conviction of any such offence; or

(3) corruptly takes any money or reward, directly or indirectly, under pretence or upon account of aiding any person to recover any stolen dog, or any dog which is in the possession of any person not being the owner thereof;

shall be guilty of a misdemeanour, and on conviction thereof liable to imprisonment for any term not exceeding eighteen months, with or without hard labour.

58 Section 5 provides special penalties for certain offences committed in respect of dogs. On general principles proof of knowledge would be required to establish unlawful possession under subsection 2.[42] The ingredients of corruptly taking a reward, in subsection 3, are dealt with more generally in section 34.[43]

40 *R v Sutton* (1838) 8 Car. & P. 291.
41 *R v Hogan* (1840) 1 Cr. & D. 366.
42 See *The People (Attorney General) v Nugent and Byrne* (1964) 98 I.L.T.R. 139; 1 Frewen 294; *Minister for Posts and Telegraphs v Campbell* [1966] I.R. 69.
43 See para. 162 *infra.*

Section 6

[LARCENY OF WILLS]

6. Every person who steals any will, codicil, or other testamentary instrument, either of a dead or of a living person, shall be guilty of felony, and on conviction thereof liable to penal servitude for life.

Section 7

[LARCENY OF DOCUMENTS OF TITLE TO LAND AND OTHER LEGAL DOCUMENTS]

7. Every person who steals the whole or any part of —

(1) any document of title to lands; or

(2) any record, writ, return, panel, petition, process, interrogatory, deposition, affidavit, rule, order, warrant of attorney, or any original document of or belonging to any court of record, or relating to any cause or matter, civil or criminal, begun, depending, or terminated in any such court; or

(3) any original document relating to the business of any office or employment under His Majesty, and being or remaining in any office appertaining to any court of justice, or in any of His Majesty's castles, palaces, or houses, or in any government or public office;

shall be guilty of felony, and on conviction thereof liable to penal servitude for any term not exceeding five years.

59 Sections 6 and 7 make provision for the stealing of certain documents which, at common law, were not capable of being stolen as they savoured of realty.[44]

44 See paras 3 and 43 *supra*.

Section 8

[DAMAGING FIXTURES, TREES, &C., WITH INTENT TO STEAL]

8. Every person who —

(1) Steals, or, with intent to steal, rips cuts severs or breaks —

    (a) any glass or woodwork belonging to any building; or

    (b) any metal or utensil or fixture, fixed in or to any building; or

    (c) anything made of metal fixed in any land being private property, or as a fence to any dwelling-house, garden or area, or in any square or street, or in any place dedicated to public use or ornament, or in any burial-ground:

(2) Steals, or, with intent to steal, cuts, breaks, roots up or otherwise destroys or damages the whole or any part of any tree, sapling, shrub, or underwood growing —

    (a) in any place whatsoever, the value of the article stolen or the injury done being to the amount of one shilling at the least, after two previous summary convictions of any such offence; or

    (b) in any park, pleasure ground, garden, orchard, or avenue, or in any ground adjoining or belonging to any dwelling-house, the value of the article stolen or the injury done exceeding the amoung of one pound; or

    (c) in any place whatsoever, the value of the article stolen or the injury done exceeding the amount of five pounds:

(3) Steals, or with intent to steal, destroys or damages any plant, root, fruit, or vegetable production growing in any garden, orchard, pleasure ground, nursery-ground, hothouse, greenhouse or conservatory, after a previous summary conviction of any such offence;

shall be guilty of felony, and on conviction thereof liable to be punished as in the case of simply larceny.

60 Section 8 alters the common law position by providing for the stealing, or damaging with intent to steal, of certain fixtures and plants. By virtue of the "new" currency which was introduced by the Decimal Currency Acts 1969 and 1970 the reference to "one shilling" in subsection 2(a) should be read as five pence.

Section 9

[LARCENY OF GOODS IN PROCESS OF MANUFACTURE]

9. Every person who steals, to the value of ten shillings, any woollen, linen, hempen or cotton yarn, or any goods or article of silk, woollen, linen, cotton, alpaca or mohair, or of any one or more of those materials mixed with each other, or mixed with any other material, whilst laid, placed or exposed, during any stage, process or progress of manufacture in any building, field or other place, shall be guilty of felony and on conviction thereof liable to penal servitude for any term not exceeding fourteen years.

61 Goods of which the texture is complete but which are not yet in a condition fit for sale are in a "stage, process or progress of manufacture".[45] However, goods which have been completed and are stored for removal do not come within the section.[46] The reference to "ten shillings" should be read as fifty pence.

Section 10

[ABSTRACTING OF ELECTRICITY]

10. Every person who maliciously or fraudulently abstracts, causes to be wasted or diverted, consumes or uses any electricity shall be guilty of felony, and on conviction thereof liable to be punished as in the case of simple larceny.

62 Given its peculiar nature, there are strong doubts as to whether electricity is "capable of being stolen".[47] Section 10, by providing for the punishment of fraudulent abstraction of electricity, avoids the problem and an offence under the section attracts the same penalty as that for simple larceny. An accused who, without authority, uses an

45 *R v Woodhead* (1836) 1 M. & Rob. 549.
46 *R v Hugill* (1800) 2 Russell on Crime (7th. ed.) 1447.
47 *Low v Blease* [1975] Crim. L.R. 513.

electrically-powered machine or implement belonging to another is guilty of the offence, as is an accused who diverts an electricity supply around the meter. A prosecution may also be brought under this section for the unauthorised use of a telephone.[48] However, an accused who passively enjoys the benefits of an electricity supply which has not been activated by him, such as by warming himself before an electric fire which has been switched on by someone else, is probably not guilty. The language employed in the section suggests active consumption on the accused's part.

63   It must be established that the abstraction was malicious or fraudulent. The inclusion of the word "maliciously" is somewhat strange, it being the only occasion that it appears in the Act. A number of possible interpretations spring to mind.[49] One is that the word "or" is conjunctive and that malice approximates fraud. A second is that malice requires an improper motive on the part of the accused, such as a desire to injure the prosecutor. A third is that "maliciously" means that the abstraction must be intentional or wilful. It is submitted that the first interpretation is to be preferred. Given that fraud is the dominant characteristic of offences under the Act[50] the adoption of a different standard here would seem to be incongruous and could lead to a curious paradox. It is established that a claim of right negatives fraud, but it would appear that it does not negative malice in the second and third senses suggested above.[51] Thus, an accused's guilt could depend on whether he was charged with maliciously abstracting or fraudulently abstracting, even though his state of mind might be the same.

64   The concept of fraud in the Act has been considered earlier and it is unnecessary to repeat that discussion.[52] It is clear that a claim of right is a defence.[53] It has been submitted that "fraudulently" should interpreted more widely than mere absence of a claim of right and that it should be equated with dishonesty and be judged according to

---

48 See also Postal and Telecommunications Services Act 1983, s. 99, which penalises the fraudulent use of telecommunications equipment.

49 See generally Edwards, *Mens Rea in Statutory Offences* (London, 1955), ch. 1.

50 See *The People (Attorney General) v Grey* [1944] I.R. 326.

51 *Gott v Measures* [1948] 1 K.B. 234; but see Edwards, *op. cit.* pp. 17-28.

52 See paras 23-29 *supra*.

53 *The People (Attorney General) v Grey* [1944] I.R. 326; *R v Bernhard* [1938] 2 K.B. 264.

contemporary social standards.[54] Of comparative interest, in this respect, is the corresponding offence of dishonestly using electricity in section 13 of the English Theft Act 1968. In *Boggeln v Williams*[55] the accused, whose electricity supply had been disconnected, informed the company of his intention to reconnect the supply. When he did this he ensured that the current passed through the meter so that his use of the electricity would be recorded. Although unauthorised, his use was held not to be dishonest.[56]

65   By virtue of section 6(1) of the Electricity (Supply) (Amendment) Act 1942 an offence under the section may be prosecuted summarily and attracts a maximum penalty of a £50 fine or six months' imprisonment. Such proceedings may, by virtue of section 6(2), be brought at the suit of either the Electricity Supply Board or any other person. That provision, in all probability, is unaffected by section 4(1) of the Criminal Justice Act 1951[57] which provides, *inter alia*, for the the summary prosecution of offences under the Larceny Act 1916, where the value of the "property" concerned does not exceed £50. It is doubtful whether electricity is "property".[58]

Section 11

[LARCENY, &C., OF ORE FROM MINES]

11. Every person who steals, or severs with intent to steal, the ore of any metal, or any lapis calaminaris, manganese, mundick, wad, black cawke, black lead, coal, or cannel coal from any mine bed or vein thereof, shall be guilty of felony and on conviction thereof liable to imprisonment for any term not exceeding two years with or without hard labour.

66   Section 11 penalises the stealing of certain ores and minerals which, by virtue of their being realty, would not otherwise be the subject of larceny.

54 See paras 26 and 29 *supra*.
55 [1978] 1 W.L.R. 873.
56 *R v Feely* [1973] Q.B. 530 applied.
57 As amended by Criminal Procedure Act 1967, s. 3, and Criminal Justice Act 1984, s. 17.
58 See the definition of "property" in section 46(1).

Section 12

12. Every person who —

    (1) steals a mail bag; or

    (2) steals from a mail bag, post office, officer of An Post, or mail, any postal packet in course of transmission by post; or

    (3) steals any chattel, money or valuable security out of a postal packet in course of transmission by post; or

    (4) stops a mail with intent to rob the mail;

shall be guilty of felony and on conviction thereof liable to penal servitude for life.

67 The words "An Post" were substituted for "the Post Office" by section 8(1) and Schedule 4 of the Postal and Telecommunications Services Act 1983. Definitions of the various expressions used in this section are contained in section 46(1). It should be noted that sections 50 to 55 of the Post Office Act 1908 contain offences in relation to stealing, embezzling and receiving postal packets.

Section 13

[LARCENY IN DWELLING-HOUSES]

13. Every person who steals in any dwelling-house any chattel, money, or valuable security shall —

    (a) if the value of the property stolen amounts to five pounds; or

    (b) if he by any menace or threat puts any person being in such dwelling-house in bodily fear;

be guilty of felony and on conviction thereof liable to penal servitude for any term not exceeding fourteen years.

68 The expressions "dwelling-house" and "valuable security" are defined in section 46.

Section 14

[LARCENY FROM THE PERSON]

14. Every person who steals any chattel, money, or valuable security from the person of another shall be guilty of felony and on conviction thereof liable to penal servitude for any term not exceeding fourteen years.

69 To amount to larceny from the person there must be a complete severance, however slight, from the person of the owner of the articles stolen. In *R v Taylor*[59] a purse, which was taken by the accused from the bottom of the owner's pocket, was caught in the lip of the pocket. It was held that although the carrying away was sufficient for the purposes of simple larceny it was not sufficient for larceny from the person. In *R v Thompson*[60] the accused took a pocket-book from the owner's inside pocket but was apprehended when it was about an inch above the pocket. His conviction was quashed as the book at all times remained about the person of the owner. However, the decision would probably have been otherwise had the book been taken from an outside pocket, as in that case it would no longer be about the person of the owner. Once there is a complete severance it is immaterial that the articles subsequently become entangled in the owner's clothing. In *R v Simpson*[61] the accused removed the owner's watch from his waistcoat pocket. In so doing, he forcibly removed the watch chain from a button-hole through which it was attached, but the chain subsequently was caught on another button. It was held that there was a sufficient severance. These decisions, which concerned the removal of articles from the owner's clothing, were accepted by the Court of Criminal Appeal in *The People (Attorney General) v Mills*[62] where the offence was held to apply equally to articles removed from a handbag which is held by the owner. Thus, once the accused succeeds in abstracting the articles completely from the handbag the offence has been committed. Moreover, it makes no difference that the accused subsequently replaces the articles in the handbag.[63]

59 [1911] 1 K.B. 674; see para. 40 *supra*.
60 (1825) 1 Mood. 80.
61 (1854) Dears. 421; see also *R v Lapier* (1784) 1 Leach 320.
62 (1955) 1 Frewen 153.
63 *Ibid.*, 155.

Section 15

15. Every person who steals —

(1) any goods in any vessel, barge or boat of any description in any haven or any port of entry or discharge or upon any navigable river or canal or in any creek or basin belonging to or communicating with any such haven, port, river, or canal; or

(2) any goods from any dock, wharf or quay adjacent to any such haven, port, river, canal, creek, or basin; or

(3) any part of any vessel in distress, wrecked, stranded, or cast on shore, or any goods, merchandise, or articles of any kind belonging to such vessel;

shall be guilty of felony and on conviction thereof liable to penal servitude for any term not exceeding fourteen years.

70   It should be noted that subsection 1 refers to stealing *in* a vessel whereas subsection 2 refers to stealing *from* a dock. Thus, where the accused is charged with larceny in a vessel it will be sufficient to show that he took the goods in the vessel, removal therefrom being unnecessary to complete the offence. However, if the accused is charged with larceny from a dock it will be necessary to prove an actual removal from the confines of the dock. Under an earlier provision[64] it was held that the goods taken must be of the type which are normally stored in a vessel or dock.[65] Whether that is still the position has yet to be decided, but as the 1916 Act is consolidating in nature the assumption must be that the older authorities apply.[66] It should be noted that section 65 of the Larceny Act 1861 provides for the punishment of a person who cannot give a satisfactory account of shipwrecked goods found in his possession. Section 66 of the same Act provides for the punishment of a person who offers shipwrecked goods for sale and who cannot show that he came by them lawfully.

---

64 24 Geo. 2 c. 45.

65 *R v Grimes* (1752) 2 East P.C. 647; see also *R v Wright* (1834) 7 Car. & P. 159.

66 The present section contains the word "goods" only, unlike earlier provisions which used expressions such as "goods, wares and merchandise" and "goods and merchandise". That difference is probably of little consequence as the term "goods" would embrace the more restricted terms.

Section 16

16. Every person who, being a tenant or lodger, or the husband or wife of any tenant or lodger, steals any chattel or fixture let to be used by such person in or with any house or lodging shall be guilty of felony and on conviction thereof liable —

(a) if the value of such chattel or fixture exceeds the sum of five pounds, to penal servitude for any term not exceeding seven years;

(b) in all other cases, to imprisonment for any term not exceeding two years, with or without hard labour;

(c) in any case, if a male under the age of sixteen years, to be once privately whipped in addition to any other punishment to which he may by law be liable.

71 This section penalises takings which would otherwise not be criminal. In *R v Meeres*[67] it was held that the tenant acquires possession of the goods for the duration of the tenancy and that, accordingly, the landlord could not maintain an action in trespass against the tenant in respect of the goods, with the consequence that the tenant could not be convicted of larceny at common law.

Section 17

17. Every person who —

(1) being a clerk or servant or person employed in the capacity of a clerk or servant —

(a) steals any chattel, money or valuable security belonging to or in the possession or power of his master or employer; or

(b) fraudulently embezzles the whole or any part of any chattel, money or valuable security delivered to or received or taken into possession by him for or in the name or on the account of his master or employer:

(2) being employed in the public service of His Majesty or in the

67 (1688) 1 Show. 50.

police of any place whatsoever —

> *(a) steals any chattel, money, or valuable security belonging to or in the possession of His Majesty or entrusted to or received or taken into possession by such person by virtue of his employment; or*
>
> *(b) embezzles or in any manner fraudulently applies or disposes of for any purpose whatsoever except for the public service any chattel, money or valuable security entrusted to or received or taken into possession by him by virtue of his employment:*

(3) being appointed to any office or service by or under a local marine board —

> *(a) fraudulently applies or disposes of any chattel, money or valuable security received by him (whilst employed in such office or service) for or on account of any local marine board or for or on account of any other public board or department, for his own use or any use or purpose other than that for which the same was paid, entrusted to, or received by him; or*
>
> *(b) fraudulently withholds, retains, or keeps back the same, or any part thereof, contrary to any lawful directions or instructions which he is required to obey in relation to his office or service aforesaid;*

shall be guilty of felony and on conviction thereof liable to penal servitude for any term not exceeding fourteen years, and in the case of a clerk or servant or person employed for the purpose or in the capacity of a clerk or servant, if a male under the age of sixteen years, to be once privately whipped in addition to any other punishment to which he may by law be liable.

72   At common law a servant who misappropriated his master's property was guilty of larceny only if the property was in the actual or constructive possession of the master.[68] Where property was entrusted by a third party to the servant on behalf of the master misappropriation by the servant was not larceny. In consequence of the decision in *R v Bazeley*[69] to this effect the offence of embezzlement was created.[70] However, the distinction between larceny by a servant and embezzlement remained. The latter offence was committed when the

---

68   *R v Reed* (1854) Dears. 168, 257; see paras 6 & 7 *supra*.

69   (1799) 2 Leach 835.

70   39 Geo. 3 c.85.

property was not in the master's possession, while the servant was guilty of larceny had the property been in the master's possession. Thus, in *R v Murray*[71] the accused who was given money by a fellow servant with instructions as to its application was not guilty of embezzlement when he misappropriated it as the money had remained in the possession of the master throughout; he should, therefore, have been charged with larceny. On the other hand, in *R v Masters*[72] the accused was held to be guilty of embezzlement where the money which he misappropriated had been given to him by a fellow servant who, in turn, had been given it by a third party to deliver to their common employer.

73   Section 17(1), which applies to clerks and servants, preserves the distinction between larceny by a servant and embezzlement. The distinction is not, however, of much contemporary practical consequence as section 44(2) of the Act allows for the substitution of verdicts. Subsection 1(a) contains the offence of larceny by a servant. This is an aggravated form of the common law offence of larceny[73] and, therefore, what has been said about larceny applies with equal force. Moreover, a servant who steals his employer's property may be prosecuted either under this provision or under section 2 of the Act.[74] Subsection 1(b) contains the statutorily-created offence of embezzlement.

74   For section 17(1) to apply it must be established that the accused was a "clerk or servant" of the owner of the property. A clerk or servant is distinguished from an officer, agent or independent contractor, whose misappropriations fall within the scope of sections 20 and 22. In essence, a clerk or servant is what nowadays is called an employee. Whether the accused falls into that category, normally is a matter for the jury.[75] Traditionally, the test applied was whether the putative master had the right to control the accused both in what he did and how he did it. An alternative way of posing the question was to ask whether the servant was obliged to act for the putative master. Thus, in *R v Negus*[76] the accused, who was engaged to work ex-

---

71   (1830) 1 Mood. C.C. 276.
72   (1848) 1 Den. 332.
73   See *The State (Foley) v Carroll* [1980] I.R. 150.
74   *Ibid*. A prosecution under s. 2 limits the sentence which may be imposed.
75   *The People (Attorney General) v Warren* [1945] I.R. 24, (1944) 78 I.L.T.R. 173.
76   (1873) L.R. 2 C.C.R. 34.

clusively for the prosecutor as a commission agent on terms which allowed him to determine whether and when he would work, was held not to be a clerk or servant. Although he was not entitled to work for anyone else the court felt that he was not bound to work for the prosecutor. Similarly, in *R v Hall*[77] the accused, who was engaged as a debt collector and to whose discretion was left the time and mode of collection, was held not to be a clerk or servant; the crucial element of control was absent. In *The People (Attorney General) v Warren*[78] the Court of Criminal Appeal held that a rate collector who was employed by Dublin Corporation was not a clerk or servant. On the other hand the relationship between the accused and the prosecutor need not be based on contract but may exist at will only; thus, a gratuitous volunteer could be held to be a clerk or servant.[79] It has also been established that a company director employed to collect money on the company's behalf may be convicted as a clerk or servant.[80] With regard to members of partnerships, section 40(4) provides for the punishment of a member who steals or embezzles property of the partnership. However, it should be noted that the practice in respect of Gardai is to prosecute under subsection 2, they being "employed in . . . the police of any place whatsoever"; the indictment usually charges the accused as "being employed as a member of the Garda Siochana". Given modern employment conditions the control test has been found to be somewhat inadequate and the trend in civil law is to adopt other criteria when determining whether a person is an employee or not.[81] Thus, factors such as the

77 (1875) 13 Cox C.C. 49.

78 [1945] I.R. 24, (1944) 78 I.L.T.R. 173.

79 *R v Foulkes* (1875) 13 Cox C.C. 63. In *Moynihan v Moynihan* [1975] I.R. 192 the defendant was held to be vicariously liable for the negligence of her daughter in the latter's capacity as a member of her household; the defendant was in a position to exercise control over the conduct of the daughter. Would the daughter be considered to be a "clerk or servant"?

80 *R v Steward* (1893) 17 Cox C.C. 723.

81 See *Cassidy v Minister for Health* [1951] 2 K.B. 343; *Stevenson, Jordan and Harrison Ltd v McDonald and Evans* [1952] T.L.R. 101; *Ready Mixed Concrete Ltd v Minister of Pensions* [1968] 2 Q.B. 497; *Ferguson v John Dawson Ltd* [1976] I.C.R. 346; *Massey v Crown Life Assurance Co* [1978] I.C.R. 590; *Young and Woods Ltd v West* [1980] I.R.L.R. 201; *McDermott v Loy* High Court, unreported, 29 July 1982; *In re Sunday Tribune Ltd* [1984] I.R. 505; *DPP v McLoughlin* [1986] I.L.R.M. 493 (though see the note by Whyte, (1986) 5 J.I.S.L.L. 144); *Kelly v Irish Press Ltd* (1986) 5 J.I.S.L.L. 17; *O'Coindealbhain v Mooney* Higher Court, unreported, 21 April 1988. See

form of remuneration, the payment of tax and social insurance, the risk of profit and loss and the ownership of equipment and materials have been taken into account. It can be expected that the criminal law will likewise broaden its definition of who is a clerk or servant.

75   Subsection 1(b) applies where the accused "fraudulently embezzles" the property in question. The decision of the Court of Criminal Appeal in *The People (Attorney General) v Grey*,[82] which considered the meaning of "fraudulently" in section 20, is of relevance to this section, as the views expressed were general in nature. The Court stated that fraud normally refers to something dishonest or morally wrong, particularly the acquisition of pecuniary or material benefits by unfair means. Although the Court did not attempt to provide an exhaustive definition, it did endorse the decision of its English counterpart in *R v Bernhard*,[83] where it was held that an unfounded claim of right was inconsistent with fraud. In an earlier decision, *R v Norman*,[84] it was held that a ship's captain who was charged with embezzling cargo could rely on a defence of claim of right.[85] Stephen, whose writing on the matter was cited in *Bernhard* and was accepted by implication in *Grey*, linked fraud with a guilty mind; fraud involves the idea of injury which is wilfully inflicted or is intended to be inflicted by deceit or secretly.[86] Although there is no direct authority on the point, it is clear that a *mens rea* element is required, either in the form of intent or knowledge of the wrongfulness of the appropriation. The improper use of the employer's property for the purpose of making money is not embezzlement; the appropriation

generally McCarthy and von Prondzynski *Employment Law* (London, 1984) pp 34- 38. In *Market Investigations Ltd v Minister of Social Security* [1969] 2 Q.B. 173 a part-time interviewer who was paid a fixed fee, without any holiday or sick pay arrangements, and who could work for other employers was held to be an employee. The authority of *R v Negus* (1873) L.R. 2 C.C.R. 34 could be called into question given the recent decisions which have reformulated the definition of an employee.

82   [1944] I.R. 326.

83   [1938] 2 K.B. 264.

84   (1842) C. & M. 501.

85   It seems to have been assumed that a ship's captain is a "clerk or servant". But although the captain's engagement has many of the incidents of employment he does stand in a special position with respect to the ship-owner. He undertakes certain fiduciary obligations and may act as agent for the owner; see Chorley and Giles, *Shipping Law* (London, 1980).

86   *History of Criminal Law*, Vol 3, p. 124: see paras 23- 29 *supra*.

must be calculated to be permanent. Thus, in *R v Callum*[87] a barge operator was held not to be guilty of embezzlement when, contrary to his instructions, he carried a load for a third party and received payment for his own account.[88]

76 The property which is alleged to have been embezzled must have been received by the accused "for or in the name or on account of" the employer. The Irish courts have not considered this element of the offence but their decisions on the equivalent, though not identical, phrase in section 20 are of assistance. It has been held that an accused receives property "for or on account of" his principal where it is received by him in circumstances which impose a binding legal obligation to pay it over or account for it.[89] The relevant relationship is that between the accused and the person to whom it is alleged he was bound to account, the perspective of the person who delivered the property being immaterial.[90] Thus, it is irrelevant that the person who delivered the property to the accused is unaware of the accused's duty to account for it to his employer. Moreover, property may be delivered on account of a person without that person's knowledge.[91] In general, where the accused is obliged to deliver to his employer property which he has received the property is received for or on account of the employer. In *R v Gale*[92] the accused cashed his employer's cheques and misappropriated the proceeds. His conviction of embezzlement of the proceeds was upheld on the ground that it was his duty, morally and legally, to deliver them to his employer.

77 The prosecution must establish a specific act or acts of misappropriation and the indictment should normally specify the individual items which it is alleged were embezzled.[93] However, it is not unusual for the prosecution to rely on circumstantial evidence in the form of deficiencies in the employer's books for which the accused was responsible. In *The People (Attorney General) v*

87 (1872) L.R. 2 C.C.R. 28.
88 If, however, the employee represents to the third party that he is acting on behalf of his employer, or within his instructions, he would probably be guilty of obtaining by false pretences. But the prosecutor would be the deceived third party.
89 *Attorney General v Lawless* [1930] I.R. 247, 259.
90 *Ibid.*, 260.
91 *The People (Attorney General) v Cowan* (1958) 98 I.L.T.R. 47.
92 (1876) 13 Cox C.C. 340.
93 *R v Tomlin* [1954] 2 All E.R. 272.

Gleeson[94] the Court of Criminal Appeal held that evidence of false entries and general deficiencies in the books can exhibit the essential ingredients of embezzlement; it is a matter for the jury to decide whether the missing amounts were embezzled by the accused. Similarly, in *The People (Attorney General) v Dalton*[95] the Court held that the jury is entitled to conclude from evidence of false entries in the employer's books that the accused took and carried away the sums concerned.[96] However, in both *Gleeson* and *Dalton* the accused was charged in respect of specific sums and strictly speaking the observations are *obiter*. But it has been held by the English Court of Criminal Appeal that a general deficiency count is permitted where it is impossible to split up an aggregate sum and to trace individual items.[97] There is no reason to suggest that an Irish court would not adopt a similar position and it has been held that a general deficiency count is permitted on a charge of fraudulent conversion.[98] Where it is impossible to establish the amount misappropriated from the deficiencies in the books the accused can alternatively be charged with falsification of accounts.[99]

78   Embezzlement may be tried summarily without any time limitation, despite provisions to the contrary in the Dublin Police Act 1842 and the Petty Sessions (Ireland) Act 1851. Those Acts were held to be incapable of limiting the jurisdiction conferred on the District Court by the Courts of Justice Act 1924.[1]

---

94   (1929) 64 I.L.T.R. 225.

95   (1960) 1 Frewen 199.

96   *Gleeson* involved a charge of embezzlement and *Dalton* one of larceny by a servant. That distinction does not however detract from the propositon that a verdict of guilty may be supported by evidence of false entries and deficiencies.

97   *R v Tomlin* [1954] 2 All E.R. 272. *R v Balls* (1871) L.R. 1 C.C.R. 328, which was followed in that case, was approved by the Court of Criminal Appeal in *The People (Attorney General) v Gleeson* (1929) 64 I.L.T.R. 225.

98   *The People (Attorney General) v Singer* (1961) 1 Frewen 214, 230 where the Court cited *R v Balls* (1871) L.R. 1 C.C.R. 328.

99   Falsification of Accounts Act 1875, s.2.

1   *Attorney General (Gordon) v Keogh* (1940) 6 Ir. Jur. Rep. 17 (decided in 1934).

Section 18

[EMBEZZLEMENT BY OFFICER OF AN POST]

18. Every person who, being an officer of An Post, steals or embezzles a postal packet in course of transmission by post shall be guilty of felony and on conviction thereof liable —

(a) if the postal packet contains any chattel, money or valuable security, to penal servitude for life:

(b) in all other cases to penal servitude for any term not exceeding seven years.

79 The words "An Post" were substituted for "the Post Office" by section 8(1) and Schedule 4 of the Postal and Telecommunications Services Act 1983, in order to accommodate the establishment of An Post by that Act. The expressions "postal packet", "in course of transmission by post" and "valuable security" are defined in section 46. In a prosecution under an earlier equivalent provision[2] it was held that proof that the accused was employed in some manner by the Post Office was necessary.[3] It should be noted that section 55 of the Post Office Act 1908 contains offences of embezzlement, stealing and destruction by postal employees.

Section 19

[EMBEZZLEMENT, &C., BY OFFICERS OF
THE BANK OF ENGLAND OR IRELAND]

19. Every person who, being an officer or servant of the Bank of England or of the Bank of Ireland, secretes, embezzles, or runs away with any bond, deed, note, bill, dividend warrant, warrant for the payment of any annuity, interest or money, security, money or other effects of or belonging to the Bank of England or Bank of Ireland and entrusted to him or lodged or deposited with the Bank of England or Bank of Ireland, or with him as such officer or servant, shall be guilty of felony and on conviction thereof liable to penal servitude for life.

2   7 Will. 4 & 1 Vict. c. 36 s. 26.
3   *R v Trenwith* (1841) 2 Cr. & D. 160.

Section 20
[CONVERSION]

20.—(1) Every person who —

(i) being entrusted either solely or jointly with any other person with any power of attorney for the sale or transfer of any property, fraudulently sells, transfers, or otherwise converts the property or any part thereof to his own use or benefit, or the use or benefit of any person other than the person by whom he was so entrusted; or

(ii) being a director, member or officer of any body corporate or public company, fraudulently takes or applies for his own use or benefit, or for any use or purposes other than the use or purposes of such body corporate or public company, any of the property of such body corporate or public company; or

(iii) being authorised to receive money to arise from the sale of any annuities or securities purchased, or transferred under the provisions of Part V. of the Municipal Corporations Act, 1882, or under any Act repealed by that Act, or under the Municipal Corporation Mortgages, &c., Act, 1860, or any dividends thereon, or any other such money as is referred to in the said Acts, appropriates the same otherwise than as directed by the said Acts or by the Local Government Board or the Treasury (as the case may be) in pursuance thereof; or

(iv) (a) being entrusted either solely or jointly with any other person with any property in order that he may retain in safe custody or apply, pay, or deliver, for any purpose or to any person, the property or any part thereof or any proceeds thereof; or

(b) having either solely or jointly with any other person received any property for or on account of any other person; fraudently converts to his own use or benefit, or the use or benefit of any other person, the property or any part thereof or any proceeds thereof; shall be guilty of a misdemeanour and on conviction thereof liable to penal servitude for any term not exceeding seven years.

(2) Nothing in paragraph (iv) of subsection (1) of this section shall apply to or affect any trustee under any express trust created by a deed or will, or any mortgagee of any property, real or personal, in respect of any act done by the trustee or morgagee in relation to the property comprised in or affected by any such trust or mortgage.

80 Section 20, which reenacts section 1 of the Larceny Act 1901, contains the offences which deal with the wrongful conversion of property by fiduciary agents. "Property" is defined in section 46 (1) of the Act. The first three paragraphs of subsection 1 deal with specific cases, whilst the fourth paragraph contains what has been described as a dragnet offence.[4] The essence of the offence is that the accused acquired the property in a fiduciary capacity and subsequently converted it wrongfully.[5] There must have been a genuine entrustment of the property to the accused in which the fiduciary ownership was obtained, but which subsequently went wrong.[6] Thus, if the accused acquires possession by way of bailment, or custody in his capacity as an employee, his conversion of the property does not come within the section, as ownership remains with the bailor or employer. The accused would be guilty of larceny by a bailee or larceny by a servant under sections 1 and 17 respectively.[7] Moreover, if the fiduciary ownership was obtained by means of a false pretence there is no genuine entrustment.[8] It is in this respect that the offence differs from that of obtaining by false pretences and the two offences are mutually exclusive,[9] although they are not infrequently charged in the alternative.

81 As stated the essence of fraudulent conversion is that the accused obtained the property in a fiduciary capacity and subsequently converted with intent to defraud. In certain cases there might be doubts as to the capacity in which the accused received the property.

4 *Attorney General v Lawless* [1930] I.R. 247.
5 *The People (Attorney General) v Singer* (1961) 1 Frewen 214; *R v Jones* (1948) 33 Cr. App. R. 11.
6 *The People (Attorney General) v Singer* (1961) 1 Frewen 214.
7 See *R v Misell* (1926) 19 Cr. App. R. 109; Russell, *Crime* (12th. ed., London, 1964) pp. 1112-1116. It should be noted that conversion by trustees and factors are dealt with in sections 21 and 22, respectively.
8 *The People (Attorney General) v Singer* (1961) 1 Frewen 214, 227.
9 *Ibid.* In *R v Jones* (1948) 33 Cr. App. R. 11 the accused obtained advance payments on contracts which he did not intend to complete. The payments were made to enable him to purchase the necessary materials. His conviction of fraudulent conversion was quashed on the grounds that the payers intended property in the money to pass to the accused and that there was no fiduciary entrustment; see also *R v Bryce* (1955) 40 Cr. App. R. 62.

In *The People (Attorney General) v Murphy*[10] the accused argued that he obtained the money as a stakeholder and not as agent for the prosecutor. The trial judge directed the jury that he obtained it as agent. The Court of Criminal Appeal considered, without deciding, the question whether that issue was one of fact to be decided by the jury or one of law to be decided by the trial judge. On the facts of the case a properly directed jury could not have failed to have found the accused to be guilty.

82   Subsection 1 (iv) is in two parts. Subparagraph (a) applies where the accused is entrusted with property for safe custody or to pay, apply or deliver it to any purpose or person. In *The People (Attorney General) v Reynolds*[11] the Court of Criminal Appeal rejected the suggestion that a fraudulent conversion of property entrusted for safe custody is different in nature from a fraudulent conversion of property entrusted for some particular purpose. Thus, where the accused is charged with the fraudulent conversion of money entrusted to him for the purpose of discharging the owner's debts it would appear that it is not a defence to show that the money was entrusted for safe custody. However, these observations are *obiter* as the Court held that the accused had in fact been entrusted with the money for the purpose of discharging the owner's debts.

83   Subparagraph (b) applies where the accused received property for or on account of another person. Whether the property was received "for or on account" is a question of fact to be determined by the jury.[12] The major statement of the law on this point is in *Attorney General v Lawless*.[13] There the Court of Criminal Appeal held that the test is whether the property was so received, and not whether property or possession passed at any moment either to the accused or to someone else. Property is received "for or on account" when it is received by the accused under circumstances which impose a binding legal obligation, arising under contract or otherwise, to pay it over or to account for it.[14] The perspective of the person who gave the property to the accused is irrelevant. In other words, the question is not whether the property was given on account of the principal but whether it was

10 (1947) 1 Frewen 85.
11 (1958) 1 Frewen 184.
12 *Attorney General v Lawless* [1930] I.R. 247; *The People (Attorney General) v Cowan* (1958) 98 I.L.T.R. 47.
13 [1930] I.R. 247.
14 *Ibid.*, 259.

received on account of the principal; it is the relationship between the accused and the person for whom it is alleged the property was received which is of relevance.[15]

84   In *The People (Attorney General) v Heald*[16] it was held that the prosecution must prove that the accused was authorised to receive the property by the person on whose account it was alleged she received the money. The accused had been engaged by a group of nuns as matron of a convalescent home run by them. She was authorised to collect and spend the patients' fees, subject to the payment of a fixed weekly sum per patient to the nuns. She arranged with two prospective patients to receive them into the home for the rest of their lives on their paying to her sums of money, which she subsequently lodged in her personal bank account. Her conviction of fraudulently converting those sums was quashed as the prosecution had failed to prove that she was authorised by the nuns to receive the money. On the other hand, it is not necessary that the owner of the property knew that it was delivered, and it has been recognised that authority to receive may be implied. In *The People (Attorney General) v Cowan*[17] the accused's client signed a bank draft at his request. It appeared that the client was unaware of the nature of the document which he signed. It was argued that, as a result of this ignorance, the client had not authorised payment of the draft. Both the Court of Criminal Appeal and the Supreme Court distinguished *Heald* and stated that the accused had an implied authority to receive the money. The circumstances of their relationship, namely that of solicitor and client, indicated that there was a duty on the accused to pay the money to the client. Lavery J considered it to be clear that if one pays money to another to be accounted for to a third person even without that person's knowledge it is received for and on his account.[18] Ó Dálaigh J said that where the owner has not authorised receipt it does not necessarily follow that the receipt was not for or on his account.[19]

85   It has been established that property which is nominally given to a corporate body can be entrusted to or received by an individual for or on account of the owner. The Court of Criminal Appeal in *The People (Attorney General) v Singer*[20] accepted as being correct the decision

15   *Ibid.*, 260.
16   [1954] I.R. 58.
17   (1958) 98 I.L.T.R. 47.
18   *Ibid.*, 53.
19   *Ibid.*, 56.
20   (1961) 1 Frewen 214.

to this effect in *R v Grubb*.[21] In the latter case the English Court of Criminal Appeal held that "being entrusted" should not be read as being limited to the moment of delivery, but may cover any subsequent period during which the accused becomes entrusted. The words "receive for or on account of" were similarly construed. The Court stated that if the accused directed and controlled the affairs of the company, and the property was passed to the company by his instruction, and he intended to defraud, he would be guilty when the property was fraudulently converted. The test is whether the accused had such control over the operation of the company that the property in reality was given to him.[22] It does not matter whether the transaction is regarded as that of the company directed and controlled by the accused, or as that of the accused using the company as an instrument to carry it out.[23] However, the jury's attention should be drawn to the material questions of fact on which such a conviction is sought to be based.[24]

86   In general the prosecution should establish a specific act, or series of acts, of misappropriation and the indictment should be framed accordingly. However, the prosecution may rely on circumstantial evidence from which a fraudulent conversion may be inferred. Proof of a duty on the part of the accused to account for property and a failure on his part to do so when required is evidence from which the jury may infer that it has been fraudulently converted.[25] In *The People (Attorney General) v A*[26] Judge Davitt considered the case of an accused who was in a precarious financial position. In those circumstances fraudulent conversion could be inferred from the accused's dealing with the property in a manner which would leave him without a reasonable prospect of accounting for it in full when required. However, the accused's unwillingness to account must not be capable of being interpreted in any other way. Thus, where a bank, without the accused's consent, transfers the surplus from one account to clear the overdraft on another, thereby making it impossible for the accused to account for the money there is no evidence to justify an inference of fraudulent conversion.[27] Moreover, it was stated in

21 [1915] 2 K.B. 683.
22 *The People (Attorney General) v Singer* (1961) 1 Frewen 214.
23 *R v Grubb* [1915] 2 K.B. 683.
24 *The People (Attorney General) v Singer* (1961) 1 Frewen 214, 225.
25 *The People (Attorney General) v Murphy* (1947) 1 Frewen 85.
26 (1941) 7 Ir. Jur. Rep. 55.
27 *Ibid.*

Singer[28] that a general deficiency count is permitted where it is impossible to trace specific items or to split the aggregate sum into identifiable amounts.[29] However, such a count is not permitted where the accused has been charged on other counts of fraudulently converting specific sums.[30]

87   The term "fraudulently" appears in paragraphs (i), (ii) and (iv) of subsection 1, but is omitted in paragraph (iii). The latter applies where the accused "appropriates the same otherwise than as directed". No doubt, *mens rea* would have to be established in regard to that offence, probably in the form of knowledge. Fraud has been considered by the Court of Criminal Appeal in *The People (Attorney General) v Grey*.[31] The Court stated that fraud connotes something dishonest or morally wrong, in particular the obtaining of a material benefit by unfair means. The Court followed *R v Bernhard*,[32] which dealt with demanding with menaces under section 30 of the Act, and held that a claim of right is a good defence to a charge of fraudulent conversion. Moreover, the Court emphasised that the claim need not necessarily be one recognised by law. An honestly made claim of right, even though unrecognised by law, is inconsistent with fraudulent conduct.

88   It has been suggested that some of the difficulties which the English courts have faced with respect to the doctrine of possession in larceny could be overcome by resorting to the offence of fraudulent conversion.[33] In particular, the suggestion is that the courts could have avoided relying on the fictions of trespassory taking[34] and postponement of "taking" to the acquisition of knowledge by the accused of the goods.[35] The proposed alternative, based on *R v Grubb*,[36] is that an accused who innocently acquires custody of goods could be held to be entrusted with them and, therefore, is guilty when he later fraudulently converts them. A problem with this suggestion

28   (1961) 1 Frewen 214.
29   *Ibid.*, 229; see also *R v Balls* (1871) L.R. 1 C.C.R. 328; *R v Lawson* [1952] 1 All E.R. 804.
30   *Ibid.*, 230.
31   [1944] I.R. 326.
32   [1938] 2 K.B. 264.
33   Edwards, "Possession and Larceny" (1950) 3 Current Legal Problems 127, 150-151.
34   *R v Riley* (1853) Dears. 149; see para. 17 *supra*.
35   *R v Ashwell* (1885) 16 Q.B.D. 190; *R v Hudson* [1943] 1 All E.R. 642; see paras 18-21 *supra*.
36   [1915] 2 K.B. 683.

is presented by the history of fraudulent conversion. It should be noted that the fictions of which the author complains were developed before the enactment of the offence. As the offence was designed to cover appropriations which hitherto were not criminal it would appear that it was not designed to apply to cases involving either a trespassory taking or postponed acquisition of possession. However, as the Irish courts have yet to consider trespassory taking and have departed from the English cases which have held that the accused does not acquire possession until he acquires knowledge of the goods,[37] it might be open to them to adopt the suggestion. Thus, the courts could be faced with two separate choices. The first is either to adopt the trespassory taking rule in *R v Riley*[38] or to apply fraudulent conversion to such cases. The second is whether or not to apply fraudulent conversion to cases which do not fall within the decision in *R v Middleton*.[39]

89   The difficulty which is presented by the application of fraudulent conversion to the cases outlined is the requirement that there be a "genuine entrustment"[40] or that the accused was authorised to receive the goods.[41] Whilst it might well be that the accused is under an obligation in civil law to account for or return the goods to the owner, it is not certain that there is either a genuine entrustment or an authority to receive. It is difficult to say that an accused in those circumstances has acquired ownership of the property subject to a fiduciary obligation owed to the prosecutor. Moreover, the fundamental distinction between passing property and possession must be borne in mind. The point made in *R v Hehir*[42] was that although property might remain with the owner possession could pass to the accused. Put another way, an accused who acquires possession does not acquire property where the owner delivers the goods under a mistake as to their characteristics. Thus, to apply fraudulent conversion to that case would seem to replace the fiction that the accused does not acquire possession with one that the accused acquires property. On the other hand some support for the suggestion is forthcoming in the acceptance in *The People (Attorney General) v Cowan*[43] that an authority to receive can be implied. However, given

37   See *R v Hehir* [1895] 2 I.R. 709.
38   (1853) Dears. 149.
39   (1873) L.R. 2 C.C.R. 38.
40   *The People (Attorney General) v Singer* (1961) 1 Frewen 214, 227.
41   *The People (Attorney General) v Heald* [1954] I.R. 58.
42   [1895] 2 I.R. 709.
43   (1958) 98 I.L.T.R. 47.

the context of the parties' relationship of solicitor and client implied authority would be self-evident. The question remains whether an owner can be said to authorise receipt where he is unaware of the goods which are delivered or where the accused is a trespasser. It is possible that the Irish courts will answer that question in the affirmative, given their acceptance of *R v Grubb*[44] and the narrow interpretation of *The People (Attorney General) v Heald*[45] in *Cowan*.

Section 21

[CONVERSION BY TRUSTEE]

21. Every person who, being a trustee as herein-after defined, of any property for the use or benefit either wholly or partially of some other person, or for any public or charitable purpose, with intent to defraud converts or appropriates the same or any part thereof to or for his own use or benefit, or the use or benefit of any person other than such person as aforesaid, or for any purpose other than such public or charitable purpose as aforesaid, or otherwise disposes of or destroys such property or any part thereof, shall be guilty of a misdemeanour and on conviction thereof liable to penal servitude for any term not exceeding seven years. Provided that no prosecution for any offence included in this section shall be commenced —

(a) by any person without the sanction of the Attorney General, or, in case that office be vacant, of the Solicitor-General;

(b) by any person who has taken any civil proceedings against such trustee, without the sanction also of the court or judge before whom such civil proceedings have been had or are pending.

90 The term "trustee" is confined to trustees of express trusts created by writing[46] and, accordingly, persons who hold property on an implied, resulting or constructive trust fall outside the provisions of the section.[47] The sanction required for a prosecution is now that of the Director of Public Prosecutions.[48]

---

44 [1915] 2 K.B. 683.
45 [1954] I.R. 58.
46 See section 46(1).
47 A trustee of a savings bank falls within the section; *R v Fletcher* (1862) L. & C. 180.
48 See Prosecution of Offences Act 1974, s. 3(1).

Section 22

22.—(1) *Every person who, being a factor or agent entrusted either solely or jointly with any other person for the purpose of sale or otherwise, with the possession of any goods or of any document of title to goods contrary to or without the authority of his principal in that behalf for his own use or benefit, or the use or benefit of any person other than the person by whom he was so entrusted, and in violation of good faith —*

    (i) Consigns, deposits, transfers, or delivers any goods or document of title so entrusted to him as and by way of a pledge, lien, or security for any money or valuable security borrowed or received, or intended to be borrowed or received by him; or

    (ii) Accepts any advance of any money or valuable security on the faith of any contract or agreement to consign, deposit, transfer, or deliver any such goods or document of title;

shall be guilty of a misdemeanour, and on conviction thereof, liable to penal servitude for any term not exceeding seven years: Provided that no such factor or agent shall be liable to any prosecution for consigning, depositing, transferring or delivering any such goods or documents of title, in case the same shall not be made a security for or subject to the payment of any greater sum of money than the amount which at the time of such consignment, deposit, transfer, or delivery, was justly due and owing to such agent from his principal, together with the amount of any bill of exchange drawn by or on account of such principal and accepted by such factor or agent.

    (2)—(a) *Any factor or agent entrusted as aforesaid and in possession of any document of title to goods shall be deemed to have been entrusted with the possession of the goods represented by such document of title.*

    (b) *Every contract pledging or giving a lien upon such document of title as aforesaid shall be deemed to be a pledge of and lien upon the goods to which the same relates.*

    (c) *Any such factor or agent as aforesaid shall be deemed to be in possession of such goods or documents whether the same are in his actual custody or are held by any other person subject to his control, or for him or on his behalf.*

(d) Where any loan or advance is made in good faith to any factor or agent entrusted with and in possession of any such goods or document of title on the faith of any contract or agreement in writing to consign, deposit, transfer, or deliver such goods or documents of title and such goods or documents of title are actually received by the person making such loan or advance, without notice that such factor or agent was not authorised to make such pledge or security, every such loan or advance shall be deemed to be a loan or advance on the security of such goods or documents of title and within the meaning of this section, though such goods or documents of title are not actually received by the person making such loan or advance till the period subsequent thereto.

(e) Any payment made whether by money or bill of exchange or other negotiable security shall be deemed to be an advance within the meaning of this section.

(f) Any contract or agreement whether made direct with such factor or agent as aforesaid or with any person on his behalf shall be deemed to be a contract or agreement with such factor or agent.

(g) Any factor or agent entrusted as aforesaid, and in possession of any goods or document of title to goods shall be deemed, for the purposes of this section, to have been entrusted therewith by the owner thereof, unless the contrary be shown in evidence.

Section 23

[ROBBERY]

23.—(1) A person is guilty of robbery if he steals, and immediately before or at the time of doing so, and in order to do so, he uses force on any person or puts or seeks to put any person in fear of being then and there subjected to force.

(2) A person guilty of robbery, or of an assault with intent to rob, shall be liable on conviction on indictment to imprisonment for life.

91 Section 23 was inserted by section 5 of the Criminal Law (Jurisdiction) Act 1976. Although the section modifies the common

law, robbery remains, in essence, larceny aggravated by circumstances of force. It must be established that the accused stole and, in order to do so, used or threatened to use force against any person. An essential element in establishing a conviction is proof that the accused stole.[49] In this context, reference must be made to the definition of stealing in section 1. It follows that the goods robbed must be "capable of being stolen".[50] Thus, if the prosecutor is compelled by force or the threat of force to endorse a valuable security in the accused's favour it is not robbery.[51] Equally, it must be established that there was a "taking", that is that the accused acquired possession of the goods. If the prosecutor merely lays down the goods and the accused is apprehended before he could pick them up there is no robbery.[52] Moreover, it is established that a claim of right is a defence even though the accused might not have believed that the means used were justified.[53]

92   The term "force" replaced "violence", which was the ingredient required in the offence under the old law. Whether the change in terminology is of any material significance is uncertain.[54] However, the English Court of Appeal has held that the corresponding offence in English law[55] was designed to overcome the technicalities which accompanied the law of larceny. In *R v Dawson and James*[56] it was stated that the trial judge, in directing the jury, should draw their attention to the words of the section and not refer to the old authorities. Whether the accused used force against any person is a question of fact to be determined by the jury based on their "common sense and knowledge of the world".[57] This approach was endorsed recently by the same court in *R v Clouden*.[58] In the former case nudging the

49 See *R v Blackburne* (1841) 2 Cr. & D. 188.

50 See paras 41-44 *supra*.

51 *R v Phipoe* (1795) 2 Leach 673; *R v Edwards* (1834) 6 Car. & P. 521. However, the accused would be guilty of some form of assault.

52 *R v Farrell* (1787) 1 Leach 322.

53 *R v Skivington* [1968] 1 Q.B. 166. The point is that the existence of a claim of right negatives the larceny which is essential. But the accused in those circumstances could be charged with an assault of the appropriate degree.

54 See *R v Dawson and James* (1976) 64 Cr. App. R. 170, 172; Smith, *The Law of Theft* (London, 1984) para. 143.

55 Theft Act 1968, s. 8.

56 (1976) 64 Cr. App. R. 170.

57 *Ibid.*, 172.

58 [1987] Crim. L.R. 56.

prosecutor so that he momentarily lost his balance was held to amount to force, as was wrenching a shopping basket from the prosecutrix's hand in the latter case. It has been suggested by English commentators that it would be preferable that the question be one of law rather than of fact, thus making the decisions uniform and not dependent on potentially variable interpretations by juries.[59] Another aspect of those decisions is that the technicalities which were associated with the old law would now seem to be inappropriate. In *Dawson and James* the court questioned the relevance of the distinction between force used to distract the prosecutor's attention and that used to overcome resistance.[60] And in *Clouden* it was expressly held that the old authorities which distinguished between force directed against the goods and force directed against the person were no longer applicable.[61] The abandonment of those technicalities is a consequence of the question's being one of fact. For instance, force which is used to distract attention could be for the purpose of stealing just as much as force used to overcome resistance. Whether such force was used in order to steal is ultimately a question of degree and fact. Technical rules which define "force" are appropriate only where the question is one of law to be ruled upon by the court. An effect of those decisions, however, is to broaden the scope of robbery and there is a considerable overlap between robbery and larceny from the person.

93   The alternative to the actual use of force is that the accused "puts or seeks to put any person in fear of being then and there subjected to force". It is clear from the wording of the section that the threat of force must be a present threat and not one as to the future. It would seem that the prosecution may seek to prove either of two forms of threat. The first is where the accused "puts . . . in fear", that is where the person threatened actually experiences fear. In that event it would be necessary to prove that fear was experienced. The second is where the accused's purpose is to put someone in fear, that is where he "seeks to put in fear". In that case it would not be necessary to establish that the person against whom the threat was directed actually was afraid. The distinction between the two is relatively unimportant as the second case would subsume the first. The requirement that the

59   Smith, *op.cit.*, para. 143; Griew, *The Theft Acts 1968 and 1978* (London, 1986) para. 3-04. Griew suggests that the court in *Clouden* interpreted *Dawson and James* as having held the question to be one of law. It is submitted that a reading of *Clouden* does not support that view.

60   (1976) 64 Cr. App. R. 170, 172.

61   [1987] Crim. L.R. 56. *R v Gnosil* (1824) 1 Car. & P. 304 not followed.

threat be made in order to steal indicates a necessary purpose on the part of the accused. Thus, an accused who put a person in fear in order to steal will have sought to put him in fear. It would follow that to charge the accused with "seeking to put in fear" would cover a case where the accused actually put someone in fear.

94   The force used or threat made must be in order to effect the stealing. Thus, proof of the accused's purpose is necessary, although in most cases that purpose will be evident from the accused's conduct and direct evidence might not be required. In other words, the jury would be entitled to infer the purpose from the circumstances of the case. However, where incidental but unrelated force is used the accused is not guilty of robbery. Thus, where an accused, who attacks the prosecutor, accepts money to desist it is not robbery.[62] In that case, however, the accused could be charged with the appropriate offence against the person and, possibly, larceny.

95   The force or threat must be at the time of or immediately before the stealing. This requirement differs somewhat from the old law which also included force used immediately after the stealing. The section provides no clues as to how immediate must be force used before the stealing. It can be presumed that the force would have to form part of the same transaction as the act of stealing and an interruption between the use of force and the stealing would negative the offence. Thus, once again, the question would seem to be one of degree to be determined by the jury as an issue of fact. A further question is whether force used after the accused has acquired possession of the goods suffices. For instance, is an accused who uses force immediately after taking the goods, in order to effect an escape, guilty of robbery? Put another way, the question is whether stealing is a momentary or a continuous act. It has been held in England, in *R v Hale*,[63] that stealing is not a momentary transaction but can be continuous. However, it is submitted that, whatever view the Irish courts might adopt, that decision could not be followed. *Hale* was concerned with stealing in the English law of theft the crucial element of which, in this context, is an appropriation by the accused. But in Ireland stealing is differently defined, in section 1, and the crucial element in the offence of larceny is a taking and carrying away.[64] The

---

62   See *R v Shendley* [1970] Crim. L.R. 49; *R v Edwards* (1843) 1 Cox C.C. 32; *R v Blackham* (1787) 2 East P.C. 711.

63   (1978) 68 Cr. App. R. 415.

64   See paras 35-40 *supra*.

Irish courts cannot ignore that definition and, thus, the English decisions are of no assistance in answering the question.[65] Instead, recourse will have to be had to the first principles of larceny, burdened as they are with technicalities which the new offence sought to avoid. It should be remembered that a taking occurs once the accused acquires possession of the goods and the carrying away need only be ever so slight.[66] Thus, an accused who removes goods and in the next instant loses possession of them is guilty of larceny. On that basis it would appear that the stealing is complete when there is a sufficient carrying away; after that the goods are stolen, not being stolen, and any force used would not be in order to steal. On the other hand, it has been held, in *Griffith v Taylor*,[67] that a power immediately to arrest a person found committing larceny could be exercised following a pursuit of the absconding thief. That decision was based on the view that the carrying away continued as long as the removal is in progress. On this view, the use of force by the accused after he has taken, but whilst he is removing, the goods would be sufficient to amount to robbery.

96   The force can be used against any person and not merely, as under the old law, against a person in possession of or in the presence of the goods. This obviates the need in cases such as *R v Harding*[68] to find that the person attacked had a "special property" in goods which are in the possession of another. The use by the accused of force to resist a passerby's attempt to prevent a larceny would complete the offence of robbery. Likewise, threatening a hostage in order to induce the owner to surrender goods would suffice. It should be noted that the force need not be used, nor the threat made, at the scene of the stealing, provided that it is contemporaneous with or immediately precedes the stealing.

97   Given the gravity of the offence, it can be presumed, on general principles, that *mens rea* as to the aggravating circumstance which converts the larceny into robbery is required. In other words, proof is necessary of a mental element with respect to the use of force or the making of a threat, as the case may be. Thus, where the accused uses force to take goods but is unaware that the force would be directed

---

65 This is a clear example of the unanticipated consequences which can result from an uncritical adoption of English statutory precedents.

66 See para. 40 *supra*.

67 (1876) 2 C.P.D. 194.

68 (1929) 21 Cr. App. R. 166; see also *Smith v Desmond* [1965] A.C. 960; and para. 15, note 57 *supra*.

against a person it is not robbery. Equally, where the accused's conduct is such that it has put a person in fear it would have to be established that the accused intended, or possibly foresaw, that his conduct would have that effect.

Section 23 (A)

[BURGLARY]

23A.—(1) A person is guilty of burglary if—

(a) he enters any building or part of a building as a trespasser and with intent to commit any such offence as is mentioned in subsection (2); or

(b) having entered any building or part of a building as a trespasser, he steals or attempts to steal anything in the building or that part of it, or inflicts or attempts to inflict on any person therein any grievous bodily harm.

(2) The offences referred to in subsection (1) (a) are offences of stealing anything in the building or part of a building in question, of inflicting on any person therein any grievous bodily harm or raping any woman therein and of doing unlawful damage to the building or anything therein.

(3) References in subsections (1) and (2) to a building shall apply also to an inhabited vehicle or vessel, and shall apply to any such vehicle or vessel at times when the person having a habitation in it is not there as well as at times when he is there.

(4) A person guilty of burglary shall be liable on conviction on indictment to imprisonment for a term not exceeding fourteen years.

98   Section 23(A), which was inserted by section 6 of the Criminal Law (Jurisdiction) Act 1976, replaced the old offence of burglary and brought the law into correspondence with that in England and Northern Ireland. The section establishes two forms of burglary: entry as a trespasser with ulterior intent, which is contained in subsection 1(a); and entry as a trespasser and committing a specified offence, which is contained in subsection 1(b). The indictment must specify the form of burglary with which the accused is charged.

99   The requirement that the accused "enters as a trespasser" replaced that of "breaking and entering" in the old law. In *Travers v Ryan*[69] it was stated that "breaking and entering" had acquired a precise legal definition as a result of case law and that the new offence is not established on proof thereof. However, where a lay witness testifies to the effect that he gave no one permission to "break into" the premises that may go to the jury as evidence of trespass on the part of the accused.[70]

100   The first element which must be established by the prosecution is that the accused entered a building or part of a building. At common law "entry" was the subject of a number of technical rules. Entry was effected where the accused placed a portion of his body, however slight, over the threshold of the dwelling. Thus, to place one's finger through a window was an entry. Moreover, if the accused inserted an implement to commit the ulterior offence he entered even though he remained physically outside the house.[71] On the other hand, use of an implement solely to gain admission did not constitute an entry.[72] The extent to which these rules have survived is uncertain. It is probable that the courts will take the view that the object of amending the law was to eliminate the old technicalities and that the term "enters" be attributed its ordinary, everyday meaning.

101   The question was touched on by the English Court of Appeal in *R v Collins*.[73] There the accused who was perched on a young woman's window sill, intending to enter her room and have intercourse with her, was invited in by her, she mistaking him for her boyfriend. He then entered the room and had intercourse with her. His conviction of burglary was overturned on the ground that it had not been established that he entered as a trespasser. It was not doubted that he had entered the room, but the question was whether he had entered before the young woman had extended her apparent invitation to him, in which case he would have entered as a trespasser. The Court stated that unless the jury was satisfied that the accused had made an "effective and substantial entry" before the apparent invitation was extended he should have been acquitted. This seems to suggest a rejection of the old technical rules, but the meaning of an "effective

69   High Court, unreported, 24 February 1984.
70   *Ibid.*
71   See Russell, *Crime* (12th. ed., London, 1964) pp. 822-825.
72   *R v Hughes* (1785) 1 Leach 406.
73   [1973] 1 Q.B. 100.

and substantial" entry is unclear. More recently, in *R v Brown*[74] the English Court of Appeal rejected the assertion that entry involves the insertion of the whole of the body into the building. The question was held to be one of fact for the jury. The Court held that what is required is an "effective" entry and it stated that the suggestion that it had to be "substantial" was unhelpful. Despite that, the matter is still unclear as the degree of intrusion which is "effective" might vary according to the circumstances of the offence charged.[75]

102   A question which remains is whether the insertion of an instrument for the purpose of committing the ulterior offence amounts to an entry. The decisions to date suggest that the courts have abandoned the old rules and replaced them with a less technical approach. Thus, attention is now focused on whether the accused made an "effective" entry, not on whether any portion of his body crossed the threshold of the building. But, those decisions concerned cases where the accused had entered the building physically and the particular matter has not yet been the subject of judicial attention. The application of the old rules could lead to strange results. It might be possible to view a grappling hook, by means of which the accused intends to steal contents from the building, as an extension of the body, the insertion of which would be an effective entry.[76] But would an accused who throws a missile through a window or sends a letter bomb intending to injure an occupant of the building be a burglar?[77] In the latter case the accused might be many miles away when the bomb arrives at the building - could he be considered to have "entered" the building?

103   With regard to the trespass requirement reference may be made to the law of tort.[78] A person trespasses where he enters either intentionally or negligently onto land without the express or implied consent of the occupier or a right of entry conferred by law. It would appear that a member of the occupier's household may give consent to the entry,[79] as may a person with a right of possession superior to that of the occupier. It can be presumed that the occupier's consent

74   [1985] Crim. L.R. 212.

75   See Smith, *The Law of Theft* (London, 1984) para. 333; Griew, *The Theft Acts 1968 and 1978* (London, 1986) para. 4-19.

76   Griew, *op. cit.*, para. 4-20a.

77   Smith, *op. cit.*, para. 344.

78   See generally McMahon and Binchy, *Irish Law of Torts* (Abingdon, 1981) ch. 24.

79   *R v Collins* [1973] 1 Q.B. 100.

may be vitiated by fraud or duress on the part of the accused.[80] Similarly, if the accused is aware that consent was the product of a mistake as to his identity consent would be vitiated, at least where identity is a material factor. In some cases a person might enjoy a right of entry until it is expressly revoked by the occupier. For instance, a member of the Garda Siochana may enter onto land to arrest someone without the express invitation of the occupier. However, on express revocation he must leave the land and becomes a trespasser if he remains.[81]

104   It would appear that a person who exceeds his right of entry is a trespasser.[82] In *R v Jones and Smith*[83] the English Court of Appeal considered the matter in relation to burglary. The two accused entered the house of the father of one of them, intending at the time to steal goods therefrom. The father testified to the effect that he had given his son an unreserved permission to enter the house and it was contended that, accordingly, the accused did not trespass. The argument was rejected and the Court was of the view that the licence to enter was subject to the unstated limitation that the accused could not enter in order to steal, which, given their intent, was the object of their entry.[84] The point was more thoroughly considered by the High Court of Australia in *Barker v The Queen*.[85] There the accused, who was asked by the occupier to mind his house while he was on vacation, entered the house and stole goods from it. The occupier testified that the accused had his authority to enter the house. The majority stated that "trespasser" is a technical word which has a particular meaning in law and it presumed that the legislature intended it to bear that meaning. If, on entry, the accused is a trespasser in the common law sense he "enters as a trespasser". A licence to enter property can be subject to express or implied limitations and, thus, where the entry exceeds those limitations it is trespassory. Applied to the facts of the case the court held that the jury was entitled to conclude that the

---

80 Under the old law access obtained by means of a false pretence was considered to be a "constructive breaking"; see *R v Finnucane* (1837) Cr. & D. (A.B.) 1.

81 See *DPP v Gaffney* [1986] I.L.R.M. 657.

82 See McMahon and Binchy *op. cit.* p. 464.

83 [1976] 3 All E.R. 54.

84 For a critique of this decision see Williams, *Textbook of Criminal Law* (London, 1982) pp. 847-850; in support of the decision see Griew, *op. cit.* paras 4-15-4-17.

85 (1983) 57 A.L.J.R. 426.

accused entered for a purpose unrelated to the permission which was conferred on him by the occupier.

105   Support for this approach would appear to be forthcoming in the Supreme Court decision in *Purtill v Athlone U.D.C.*[86] where Walsh J accepted, *obiter*, that a licensee who forms intent to steal after entry becomes a trespasser.[87] It would follow that if the licensee enters with intent he enters as a trespasser. On this reckoning it would seem that a person who enters a store on a shoplifting expedition enters as a trespasser with intent to steal and, therefore, is a burglar. On the other hand, a shopper who steals after he has entered innocently would not be a burglar because he has not entered as a trespasser. There is nothing in *R v Jones and Smith* to dispute that proposition, but it should be noted that in *Purtill* the plaintiff's status was not material to the decision and that the Court was not concerned with the interpretation of the phrase "entry as a trespasser". Moreover, despite the similarity between *Jones and Smith* and *Barker*, *dicta* in the latter suggest that the position of the shoplifter would be different. Mason J thought that the shoplifter would enter with the permission of the owner and the fact that the owner would not have extended a licence had he been aware of the accused's purpose is immaterial — "it is the effect of the licence actually given that is decisive".[88] Brennan and Deane JJ thought that if the general permission has not been expressly or impliedly limited it may not be "cut back" because, had the matter been raised, the owner would have qualified its scope.[89] Thus, the relevant question focuses on the actual permission given, not on that which would have been given had the occupier been endowed with the benefit of foresight. In *Barker* the permission was to enter the house for the purpose of minding it and no other. But in *Jones and Smith* the evidence was that the father had given a general permission to enter which would suggest that the court "cut back" the accused's unqualified licence. In this respect the two decisions differ and are difficult to reconcile.[90]

106   Although the trespass requirement overlaps substantially with the civil law on trespass the two are not wholly congruent. It has been stated that the civil doctrine of trespass *ab initio* has no place in the

86 [1968] I.R. 205.
87 *Ibid.*, 210.
88 (1983) 57 A.L.J.R. 426, 430.
89 *Ibid.*, 433-436.
90 *Ibid.*, 429, 435.

criminal law.[91] Thus, one cannot retrospectively enter as a trespasser. More significantly, it was held in *Collins* that the accused must either know that his entry is trespassory or be reckless as to that fact. Thus, where the accused entered the room on the young woman's invitation, which was based on her mistaking his identity, it was incumbent on the prosecution to prove knowledge or recklessness on his part as to the absent of consent. In *Jones and Smith* it was stated that the effect of *Collins* was to add a *mens rea* requirement to the civil law concept of trespass. If an accused is aware of, or reckless as to, facts which enable him to realise that he enters in excess of the licence conferred on him by the occupier he is a trespasser for the purposes of burglary.[92] This proposition applies equally to express and implied limitations. In both *Jones and Smith* and *Barker* the limitation was implied yet the accused, in effect, were held to have been aware of it.

107   The entry must be into a "building or part of a building". Subsection 3 includes inhabited vehicles and vessels within the definition of a building. Other than that the section gives no clues as what is a "building". The preponderant view is that a building is a relatively permanent structure.[93] Thus, an erection which consists of walls and a roof would be a building. It is impossible to predict the outcome of borderline cases such as telephone kiosks, bandstands, greenhouses, garden sheds or ruined castles. There are however two marginally-reported English cases on the question. In *B & S v Leathley*[94] a freezer container resting on old railway sleepers was held to be a building it being "a structure of considerable size and intended to be permanent or at least to endure for a considerable time".[95] In *Norfolk Constabulary v Seekings and Gould*[96] articulated truck trailers which were supplied with electricity and used as temporary storage space were held not to be buildings. With regard to inhabited vehicles and vessels it is clear that they can be burgled even though the inhabitant is not present at the time of entry. However, it would seem that a vehicle or vessel can cease to be inhabited or even be inhabited for certain periods only. For instance, a camper van which is lived in by the owner during vacation might be used as a motor car

91   *R v Collins* [1973] 1 Q.B. 100; *Barker v The Queen* (1983) 57 A.L.J.R. 426.
92   [1976] 3 All E.R. 54, 59.
93   See Smith, *op. cit.* para. 343; Griew, *op. cit.* para. 4-21.
94   [1979] Crim. L.R. 314.
95   *Ibid.*
96   [1986] Crim L.R. 167.

for the rest of the year. It is submitted that it would be an "inhabited vehicle" during vacation, but would cease to be so when it reverts to "ordinary" use.[97]

108   The interpretation of "part of a building" is no less easy. It can be presumed that permanent divisions in a building, such as walls and doors, demarcate separate parts of a building. However, temporary divisions, such as moveable screens, ropes or "no entry beyond this point" notices, could raise different considerations. If such divisions were deemed to segregate it into separate parts, a building, because of their impermanence, would vary as to its component parts from time to time. In that case, the accused's guilt would depend not on his "real" culpability, or the evil which is perceived to be implicit in burglary, but on whether someone had placed a screen in the appropriate place, a fortuitous circumstance which might seem out of place in the criminal law. A test was suggested by the English Court of Appeal in *R v Walkington*[98] where a rectangular counter area in a store, made up of a three-sided moveable counter, was held to be "part of a building". The Court noted that there was a physical partition and said that it was a question for the jury to determine whether it was "sufficient to amount to an area from which the public were plainly excluded".[99] But the court did note that it would be difficult to conclude that a single table placed in the middle of the floor was a part of the building.[1]

109   Greater difficulty might be experienced where a building, such as an apartment block, is divided into a number of identifiable parts. Clearly the entire block is a "building" and an accused who, from the outside, enters one apartment as a trespasser in order to gain access to other apartments, where he intends to steal, is guilty of burglary. But suppose that the accused, who lawfully enters one apartment, is apprehended when trespassing in a second in order to gain access to a third, where he intends to steal. If the second and third apartments are separate "parts" he is not guilty of burglary as he has not entered the part in which he intended to steal. Smith has suggested that to deal with such a case a building should be considered to consist of two parts, that into which the accused may lawfully go and that from

97 See Smith, *op. cit.*, para. 353.
98 [1979] 1 W.L.R. 1169.
99 *Ibid.*, 1176.
1   *Ibid.*

which he is excluded.[2] Thus, all the apartments other than that in which the accused's presence is lawful constitute one part. Despite its superficial attraction, the theory poses considerable difficulties. The example given can be made even more improbable. Suppose that while the accused is engaged in his larcenous enterprise another miscreant, who is lawfully in the twenty-first apartment, is apprehended when trespassing in the twenty-second in order to gain access to the twenty-third. Applying Smith's theory the second accused also has entered "part of a building" with intent to steal therein. Now the building consists of four parts all of which overlap considerably, and the parts of the building will multiply as more entrants with intent to steal arrive! A more probable difficulty arises when this theory is applied to *R v Jones and Smith*.[3] Suppose that a shopper, having lawfully entered a shop, decides to steal. He now becomes a trespasser and his duty is to leave the premises by the most convenient route. Instead, however, he proceeds towards consummation of his undisclosed desire and takes one step in the opposite direction. On Smith's theory it would now seem that he has entered a part of the building as a trespasser with intent to steal therein. That curious conclusion is tantamount to bringing the discredited doctrine of trespass *ab initio* in through the back door. It is submitted, therefore, that "parts of a building" should be physically identifiable and that the question which the courts will have to determine is whether the physical partition must be permanent or whether, as *R v Walkington*[4] suggests, temporary partitions would be sufficient.

110   As noted earlier burglary can be committed in either of two ways. The first is that the accused enters as a trespasser with intent to steal, rape, inflict grievous bodily harm or do unlawful damage; and the second is that the accused enters as a trespasser and steals or attempts to steal or inflicts or attempts to inflict grievous bodily harm. With respect to entry with ulterior intent it has been held in England that a "conditional" intent to steal (i.e. an intent to steal only those objects worth stealing) can be sufficient. In *R v Walkington*[5] the English Court of Appeal upheld a conviction of burglary by entering with intent to steal even though, unknown to the accused, there was nothing to steal

---

2   Smith, *op. cit.*, paras. 347, 350; Griew, *op. cit.*, para. 4-23, considers the interpretation to be "desirable but strained".

3   [1976] 3 All E.R. 54.

4   [1979] 1 W.L.R. 1169.

5   *Ibid.*

81

in the particular part of the building.[6] The matter was again considered by the same court in *Re Attorney-General's References (Nos. 1 and 2 of 1979)*[7] where *Walkington* was approved. The Court distinguished *R v Easom*[8] on the ground that the indictment in that case specified the items which were the subject matter of the charge. In *Walkington*, however, particular items were not specified; the indictment alleged an intent to steal simpliciter. Therefore, it would appear that a "conditional" intent is sufficient where the indictment does not specify particular items which it is alleged the accused intended to steal. On principle the same reasoning ought to apply to the other offences which it is alleged the accused intended to commit on entry. Thus, an accused who enters a building intending to have intercourse with a woman therein, whether or not she consents, or whether or not a woman is in fact present, would be guilty of burglary.

111   "Stealing" for the purposes of the section must be interpreted with reference to the definition in section 1. The things stolen, or which the accused intended to steal, must be "capable of being stolen".[9] Thus, an accused who steals, or intends to steal, title deeds or electricity would not be guilty of burglary. In a similar vein, the existence of a genuinely held claim of right on the part of the accused would preclude a conviction of burglary.[10] The definition of "rape" in section 2(1) of the Criminal Law (Rape) Act 1981 will govern the interpretation of intent to rape for the purposes of burglary. Subsection 2 refers to offences which include doing "unlawful damage to the building or anything therein". Hence it will not be enough to show that the accused intended cause damage which is merely tortious. The section does not further identify the offences in mind and presumably an intent to do any damage which would amount to a crime will be sufficient. In practice, the offences most commonly intended by an accused will be arson and offences under the Malicious Damage Act 1861.

112   Subsection 1(b) refers to the infliction of grievous bodily harm whilst subsection 2 refers to offences of inflicting grievous bodily harm. This raises the possibility that a charge of burglary by entry and inflicting need not involve an *offence* of grievous bodily harm. Thus,

6   *R v Greenhoff* [1979] Crim. L.R. 108 overruled.
7   [1980] Q.B. 80.
8   [1971] 2 Q.B. 315; see para. 46 *supra*.
9   See paras 41-44 *supra*.
10 *The People (Attorney General) v Grey* [1944] I.R. 326; *R v Bernhard* [1938] 2 K.B. 164.

an accused who might have a defence to a charge of grievous bodily harm could possibly be convicted of burglary. On the other hand, an accused who is charged with burglary by entry with intent would be acquitted if he believed in the existence of facts which would justify the infliction of grievous bodily harm.[11] It is, however, probable that the omission of the word "offence" in subsection 1(b) is of little consequence and that both subsections refer to offences.[12] Inflicting grievous bodily harm is an offence under section 20 of the Offences Against the Person Act 1861 and in *R v Jenkins*[13] the English Court of Appeal held that the words should bear the same meaning in reference to burglary.[14] Thus, where an accused is charged with burglary by entry and inflicting it is necessary for the prosecution to prove conduct on the part of the accused which, in itself, would amount to an offence under section 20. The court also held that "inflicting" was wider than an "assault" and that an accused charged with burglary by entering and inflicting could not be convicted of assault occasioning actual bodily harm under section 47 of the Act of 1861.[15] Although the matter was not considered in *Jenkins*, it can be presumed that "inflicting grievous bodily harm" would embrace an offence under section 23 of the Offences Against the Person Act 1861[16] and greater offences, such as murder, which necessarily incorporate an offence under section 20 of that Act.[17] In *The People (Attorney General) v Messitt*[18] the Supreme Court adopted the House of Lords decision in *DPP v Smith*[19] which defined "grievous bodily

11 See *R v Gladstone Williams* (1984) 78 Cr. App. R. 276.
12 Smith, *op. cit.*, para. 359, states that the omission of the word "offence" from the equivalent English provision was a legislative accident. Is it not a strange coincidence that the Oireachtas met with the same accident?
13 [1983] 1 All E.R. 1000.
14 *Ibid.*, 1005.
15 *Ibid.* This part of the decision was overturned by the House of Lords on different grounds which involved the interpretation of the English Criminal Law Act 1967, s. 6(3); see *R v Jenkins* [1983] 3 All E.R. 448. The equivalent Irish provisions are contained in ss. 29 and 34 of the Courts of Justice Act 1924 and s. 12(2) of the Courts (Supplemental Provisions) Act 1961; see *The People (Attorney General) v Messitt* [1974] I.R. 406, 414; see also Ryan and Magee, *The Irish Criminal Process* (Cork, 1983) pp. 429-432.
16 S. 23 prohibits inflicting grievous bodily harm by administering poison.
17 See Smith and Hogan, *Criminal Law* (London, 1983) p. 567.
18 [1974] I.R. 406.
19 [1961] A.C. 290.

harm" as meaning really serious harm. In *R v Miller*[20] "bodily harm" was said to include any hurt calculated to interfere with the health or comfort of the prosecutor and included mental as well as physical injuries.

Section 23 (B)

[AGGRAVATED BURGLARY]

23B.—(1) A person is guilty of aggravated burglary if he commits any burglary and at the time has with him any firearm or imitation firearm, any weapon of offence or any explosive; and, for this purpose—

> *(a) "firearm" includes an airgun or air pistol, and "imitation firearm" means anything that has the appeareance of being a firearm, whether capable of being discharged or not;*
>
> *(b) "weapon of offence" means any article made or adapted for use for causing injury to or incapacitating a person, or intended by the person having it with him for such use; and*
>
> *(c) "explosive" means any article manufactured for the purpose of producing a practical effect by explosion, or intended by the person having it with him for that purpose.*

(2) A person guilty of aggravated burglary shall be liable on conviction on indictment to imprisonment for life.

113   Section 23(B) was inserted by section 7 of the Criminal Law (Jurisdiction) Act 1976. In essence the offence is that of burglary, aggravated by the accused's having with him a firearm, weapon or explosive at the time of the burglary.[21] It can be presumed that the evil which the Oireachtas had in mind when enacting the offence was the additional threat of violence to occupants posed by the presence of weapons.

114   For purposes of the offence the expressions "firearm", "imitation firearm", "weapon of offence" and "explosive" are elaborated in paragraphs (a), (b) and (c) of subsection 1. In this context it is

20   [1954] 2 All E.R. 529.
21   See generally Smith, *The Law of Theft* (London, 1984) paras. 362-376; Griew, *The Theft Acts 1968 and 1978* (London, 1986) paras. 4-32-4-42.

interesting that the Oireachtas did not incorporate the definitions of "firearm" and "imitation firearm" which are contained in the Firearms Acts 1925-1971.[22] It would follow therefore that "firearm" should bear its natural meaning and not that ascribed to it by the Firearms Acts. This view is reinforced by the express inclusion of airguns and air pistols within the meaning of the term "firearm"; that inclusion would be unnecessary if the term was to bear the meaning attributed to it in the Firearms Acts.[23] Thus, it is submitted that component parts of a firearm, which are deemed to be "firearms" for the purposes of the Firearms Acts 1925-1971,[24] are not firearms for purposes of the section. However, a component part might be an "imitation firearm" where it resembles a firearm. For instance, an accused who holds the detached barrel of a gun in such a manner as to conceal its nature could be held to possess an imitation firearm. Whether the thing has the appearance of a firearm would be a question of fact to be determined by the jury.

115   "Weapon of offence" incorporates three categories: articles which are made for causing injury to or incapacitating a person; articles which are adapted for causing injury to or incapacitating a person; and articles which the accused intends to use for causing injury to or for incapacitating a person. It appears that the inclusion of incapacitation as a purpose brings within the section articles which can be used to disable a person without injuring him, such as ropes used for binding a person.[25] The definition of "weapon of offence" closely resembles that of "offensive weapon" in the British Prevention of Crime Act 1953,[26] and the decisions under that Act are of some assistance. Those decisions have distinguished between weapons which are offensive *per se* and those which are not.[27] The former are "made" for the purpose of causing injury, whereas the

22 See Firearms Act 1925, s. 1(1); Firearms Act 1964, s 2(1); Firearms Act 1971, s. 2.

23 Firearms Act 1964, s. 2(1) brings airguns within the definition of "firearms" in the Acts. "Firearm" in s. 12 of the Licensing Act 1872 includes air rifles; see *Seamark v Prouse* [1980] 1 W.L.R. 678.

24 Firearms Act 1971, s. 2.

25 See Smith, *op. cit.* para. 364.

26 S. 1(4) of that Act defines "offensive weapon" as being "any article made or adapted for use for causing injury to the person, or intended by the person having it with him for such use".

27 See Smith and Hogan, *Criminal Law* (London, 1983) pp. 396-401; Smith, *op. cit.* para. 364; Griew *op. cit.* paras. 4-35-4-39.

latter are either "adapted" or "intended" for such use. A court can take judicial notice that the thing was made for the purpose of causing injury. Thus, in *R v Simpson*[28] judicial notice was taken of the fact that a flick knife is made for that purpose. Moreover, the fact that a weapon can be used for innocent purposes does not take it out of that category.[29] Other items of which judicial notice could similarly be taken include knuckledusters, coshes, bayonets, stilettos and daggers. On the other hand, articles like sheath knives[30] and tools[31] are not offensive *per se* and the question whether they are adapted or intended for use is one of fact to be resolved by the jury. An adaptation necessarily involves some alteration to the article, a common example given being that of a bottle broken so that the jagged end can be used for stabbing.[32] Thus, an unaltered article, such as a screwdriver, which is used by the accused to injure a person is not adapted. And, as quite clearly it has not been made for the purpose of causing injury, the prosecution would have to show that it was intended for such use by the accused in order to establish that it was a "weapon of offence". Where it is alleged that the article was intended for use by the accused it appears to be necessary to establish that the intention was premeditated, in the sense that the accused had that purpose in mind before the occasion for use arose.[33] If, however, in the heat of the moment, the accused uses the article to cause injury it does not become a "weapon of offence".[34] Thus, a burglar, who is surprised by the occupier and stabs him with a screwdriver which he brought with him to open the safe, would not be guilty of aggravated burglary as the use of that article would have occurred in the heat of the moment.

116   It is must be established that the accused had the article of aggravation with him at the time of the burglary. The use of the phrase "has with him" rather than "in his possession" indicates that the prosecution must establish something more than possession. In *R v Kelt*[35] it was held that the same expression in the British Firearms Act 1968 requires a close physical link and immediate control. However,

28 [1983] 1 W.L.R. 1494; see also *Gibson v Wales* [1983] 1 W.L.R. 393.
29 *Ibid.*, 1497.
30 *R v Williamson* (1977) 67 Cr. App. R. 35.
31 *R v Petrie* [1961] 1 All E.R. 466.
32 *R v Simpson* [1983] 1 W.L.R. 1494, 1496.
33 *Ohlson v Hylton* [1975] 1 W.L.R. 724.
34 *Wood v Commissioner of Police of the Metropolis* [1986] 1 W.L.R. 796.
35 [1977] 1 W.L.R. 1365.

it is not necessary to show that the accused was carrying the article and the question is one of fact and degree.[36] In practice, there will probably be few cases in which an accused has an article with him without carrying it. One possible case would be where a confederate deposits the article for the accused on the premises in advance of the burglary; sufficient physical proximity might be established without an actual touching of the article. On general principles, knowledge on the part of the accused of the existence of the article is necessary.[37] The section is silent, however, as to whether knowledge of the article's character would be required. It is submitted that, given the gravity of the offence, the presumption that *mens rea* is required for each element of an offence should be applied.[38] Therefore it would be necessary to show that the accused was aware of the article's character or at least reckless thereto.[39]

117   The time of the offence will depend on the form of burglary which it is alleged the accused committed. If the burglary alleged is by entering as a trespasser with intent the offence is complete on entry and, therefore, it must be proven that the accused had the article of aggravation with him at the time of the entry. If, on the other hand, the burglary alleged is entry as a trespasser and committing the offence is complete on the commission of the ulterior offence and the relevant time is that of the commission. Thus, where an accused, who enters unarmed, finds a weapon in the building and has it with him when he commits an ulterior offence he is guilty of aggravated burglary.[40] However, in that case it is crucial that the burglary charged is entry and committing, not entry with intent.[41]

---

36 *Ibid.*, 1369.

37 *R v Cugullere* [1961] 2 All E.R. 343; *The People (Attorney General) v Nugent and Byrne* (1964) 98 I.L.T.R. 139; *Minister for Posts and Telegraphs v Campbell* [1966] I.R. 69.

38 *The People (DPP) v Murray* [1976] I.R. 360.

39 See *contra Warner v Metropolitan Police Commissioner* [1969] 2 A.C. 256. That decision would probably not apply as it concerned possession of drugs which could be regarded as being *sui generis*; in any event, it has not been followed in this jurisdiction and seems to be inconsistent with *The People (DPP) v Murray* [1976] I.R. 360.

40 *R v O'Leary* (1985) 82 Cr. App. R. 341.

41 See *contra* Griew, *op. cit.* para. 4-42.

Sections 24-27

118 Sections 24 to 27, inclusive, were repealed by section 21(1) of the Criminal Law (Jurisdiction) Act 1976. Those sections were rendered otiose by the creation of the new offence of burglary, in section 23(A), which embraces the conduct proscribed by the repealed sections. It should be noted that section 21(7) of the 1976 Act provides for cases where the accused is charged in the alternative with an offence under the repealed sections and with burglary or aggravated burglary under sections 23(A) or 23(B). If it is established that the accused committed acts which amount to the offences charged, but it is uncertain whether the acts were done before or after the commencement of the 1976 Act, he may be convicted of the offence under the repealed provision. However, the accused will be liable to the lesser of the maximum penalties for the two offences charged.

Section 28

[BEING FOUND BY NIGHT, ARMED OR IN POSSESSION OF HOUSE-BREAKING IMPLEMENTS]

28. Every person who shall be found by night —

(1) armed with any dangerous or offensive weapon or instrument, with intent to commit any burglary; or

(2) having in his possession without lawful excuse (the proof whereof shall lie on such person) any key, picklock, crow, jack, bit, or other implement of house-breaking; or

(3) having his face blackened or disguised with intent to commit any felony; or

(4) in any building with intent to commit any felony therein;

shall be guilty of a misdemeamour and on conviction thereof liable—

(a) if he has been previously convicted of any such misdemeanour or of any felony, to penal servitude for any term not exceeding ten years;

(b) in all other cases, to penal servitude for any term not exceeding five years.

119   The offences contained in this section are directed principally against acts which are preparatory to burglary. To reflect the new definition of burglary section 21(3) of the Criminal Law (Jurisdiction) Act 1976 inserted the words "commit any burglary" in substitution for words which were based on the old requirement of breaking and entering. However, in two other respects section 28 was not altered to reflect the changes in the law of burglary. The first is that the offences in this section consist of being found at night[42] although burglary is no longer confined to that time. Thus, a person who commits preparatory acts during daytime does not come within the section, even though he could be found guilty of the full offence. The second is the retention of the phrase "implement of house-breaking", in subsection 2, rather than its replacement by "implement of burglary". Under the old law burglary consisted of breaking and entering a dwelling house and, therefore, an article used for burglary was a house-breaking implement. However, in this context burglary is now a wider offence which can be committed in respect of any building and it is possible that an instrument of burglary might not be an "implement of house breaking".

120   Subsection 1 applies where the accused is found armed with a "dangerous or offensive weapon or instrument", which, by virtue of section 25(1) of the Firearms Act 1964, includes unloaded and imitation firearms. Other than that the expression is not defined. This contrasts with "weapon of offence" in section 23(B) which is defined as an article made, adapted or intended for causing injury.[43] However, that definition is of no assistance to the interpretation of the present section.[44] When it enacted section 23(B) the Oireachtas chose a phrase which is new to the Act and defined that phrase. It declined the opportunity to use the existing phrase or to amend the words used in section 28. Accordingly, it would appear that the things to which subsection 1 refers are those which are intrinsically dangerous or offensive. They would include firearms, knives, knuckledusters and coshes, but would exclude implements such as screwdrivers which could be used for causing injury. To complete the offence it must be shown that the accused had an intent to commit burglary. That intent

---

42 Defined in section 46(1) as being between 9.00 p.m. and 6.00 a.m.

43 See para. 115 *supra*.

44 Equally, the interpretation of "offensive weapon" in the British Prevention of Crime Act 1953, s. 1(4) is of no help as its definition is similar to that of "weapon of offence"; see para. 115, note 26 *supra*.

will consist of an intent to enter a building as a trespasser with specific intent.[45] Proof of knowledge on the part of the accused of the trespassory nature of the intended entry is necessary.[46] It has been held in a charge under the similar provision in section 58 of the Larceny Act 1861 that the prosecution must prove an intent to commit burglary in a particular building.[47] On this basis proof of a general intent to commit burglary in an unspecified building would be insufficient. But if the prosecution can establish an intent to enter a particular building the fact that the accused had a conditional intent to steal only those items which appeal to him does not negative the intent to commit burglary.[48]

121   Subsection 2 applies where the accused is found in possession of certain specified objects without lawful excuse. The extent to which the general law of possession applies is uncertain. It has been held that possession of implements by one housebreaker amounts to possession by his accomplices. But the mere fact that the accused is in the company of a person who in fact is in possession of implements does not establish the offence.[49] Some degree of control over the implements by the accused would have to be established.[50] It is submitted that the possession to which the provision refers is immediate possession. A person can possess objects which are not in his immediate presence, such as when they are in his house or in the custody of a confederate.[51] However, an accused who is in possession of goods which are stored in his home could hardly be said to be "found in possession" when apprehended in the street. Moreover, such possession could not be considered to be an act preparatory to burglary and is beyond the mischief contemplated by section 28.

122   The prohibited objects must be for the purpose of housebreaking and intended for that use; it is for the jury to determine whether the

45 See paras 110-112 *supra*.
46 See *R v Collins* [1973] 1 Q.B. 100; *R v Jones and Smith* [1976] 3 All E.R. 54.
47 *R v Jarrald and Ost* (1863) 9 Cox C.C. 307.
48 See *Re Attorney-General's References (Nos. 1 and 2 of 1979)* [1980] Q.B. 180; but see *contra R v Easom* [1971] 2 Q.B. 315.
49 *R v Lester and Byast* (1955) 39 Cr. App. R. 157; *R v Harris* [1961] Crim. L.R. 256.
50 See *Minister for Posts and Telegraphs v Campbell* [1966] I.R. 69; *The People (Attorney General) v Nugent and Byrne* (1964) 98 I.L.T.R. 139; *The People (Attorney General) v Kelly and Robinson* (1953) 1 Frewen 147.
51 *Ibid.*

implements were intended for that purpose.[52] It would appear that the general expression "implement of house-breaking" is to be widely interpreted; thus, a brick has been held to be an implement of housebreaking.[53] A misdescription in the indictment of the implement which is found in the accused's possession is not fatal provided that it does not affect the substance of the indictment.[54] It should be noted that the implements in question must be for the purpose of house-breaking, not of burglary. Given the relevance of the accused's intent with respect to the implements found it his possession it would seem that possession of implements for a burglary which would not have amounted to house-breaking under the old law is not an offence. This follows from the omission to alter the words of the subsection to accommodate the newly-defined offence of burglary.

123   The existence of lawful excuse on the part of the accused raises a question as to the onus of proof which has been the subject of conflicting decisions in England. In *R v Ward*[55] it was held that proof by the accused that the implements were the tools of his trade was sufficient to shift the onus of establishing absence of lawful excuse to the prosecution. That decision was disapproved in *R v Patterson*[56] where it was held that the accused bears the burden of proving lawful excuse on the balance of probabilities once the prosecution establishes that the implements were capable of being used for house-breaking. It is submitted that *Ward* is to be preferred as it reflects the general principle which places the burden of proof on the prosecution. Thus, once the accused establishes the existence of circumstances which are capable of amounting to a lawful excuse the onus of negativing that inference rests with the prosecution.

124   The offences in this section may be tried summarily.[57]

---

52 *R v Oldham* (1852) 2 Den. 472.
53 *R v Loney* [1956] Crim. L.R. 494.
54 *The People (Attorney General) v Hayden* (1970) 1 Frewen 347.
55 [1915] 3 K.B. 696.
56 [1962] 2 Q.B. 429.
57 S. 2, Schedule 1 Criminal Justice Act 1951, as amended by s. 19(2)(a) of the Criminal Procedure Act 1967.

Section 29

29.—*(1) Every person who—*

    (i) utters, knowing the contents thereof, any letter or writing demanding of any person with menaces, and without any reasonable or probable cause, any property or valuable thing;

    (ii) utters, knowing the contents thereof, any letter or writing accusing or threatening to accuse any other person (whether living or dead) of any crime to which this section applies, with intent to extort or gain thereby any property or valuable thing from any person;

    (iii) with intent to extort or gain any property or valuable thing from any person accuses or threatens to accuse either that person or any other person (whether living or dead) of any such crime;

shall be guilty of felony, and on conviction thereof liable to penal servitude for life, and, if a male under the age of sixteen years, to be once privately whipped in addition to any other punishment to which he may by law be liable.

    (2) Every person who with intent to defraud or injure any other person—

    (a) by any unlawful violence to or restraint of the person of another, or

    (b) by accusing or threatening to accuse any person (whether living or dead) of any such crime or of any felony,

compels or induces any person to execute, make, accept, endorse, alter, or destroy the whole or any part of any valuable security, or to write, impress, or affix the name of any person, company, firm or co-partnership, or the seal of any body corporate, company or society upon or to any paper or parchment in order that it may be afterwards made or converted into or used or dealt with as a valuable security, shall be guilty of felony and on conviction thereof liable to penal servitude for life.

    (3) This section applies to any crime punishable with death, or penal servitude for not less than seven years, or any assault with intent to commit any rape, or any attempt to commit any rape, or any solicitation, persuasion, promise, or threat offered or made to any

person, whereby to move or induce such person to commit or permit the abominable crime of buggery, either with mankind or with any animal.

(4) For the purposes of this Act it is immaterial whether any menaces or threats be of violence, injury, or accusation to be caused or made by the offender or by any other person.

125   Sections 29 to 31, which contain the law on what is colloquially termed "blackmail", have been described as "an ill-assorted collection of legislative bric-a-brac which the draftsman . . . put together with scissors and paste".[58] The sections represent the collation of a series of piecemeal statutory provisions which were enacted from the eighteenth century onwards.[59] Moreover, certain forms of blackmail amounted to robbery at common law, in particular extortion by threatening to accuse the prosecutor of having engaged in "unnatural practices".[60] There still remains an overlap between the offences contained in these sections and those of robbery and assault with intent to rob, although its extent has not been accurately identified. The uncertainty is aggravated by an element of inconsistency in the authorities and in Ireland matters are further confused by a dearth of reported cases, which we might flatteringly believe to be a reflection of the national character. The gravamen of the offences contained in these sections is the making of improper threats in order to gain some benefit.

126   Section 29 contains a number of separate, but overlapping, offences, each of which attracts a punishment of penal servitude for life. Subsection 1 contains three offences: uttering a letter or writing demanding with menaces; uttering a letter which accuses or threatens to accuse a person of a crime; and accusing or threatening to accuse a person of a crime. The first offence is general in nature, being concerned with demands with menaces, while the second and third offences are concerned with the making of accusations or threats of accusation with intent to extort. The first and second offences, but not the third, require the uttering of a letter, the accused having knowledge of the contents; thus, it need not be established that the prosecutor received the letter, much less that he acted on it. Subsection 2 applies where the accused compels or induces a person to deal with certain

---

58   Hogan, "Blackmail: Another View" [1966] Crim. L.R. 474.
59   See para. 10 *supra.*
60   See *R v Pollock and Divers* [1966] 2 All E.R. 97 and cases cited therein.

documents or valuable securities. This may be achieved by either of two means: unlawful violence to, or restraint of, the person of another; and accusation or threat of accusation of a crime. The crimes to which the accusation refer are listed in subsection 3.[61] "Property" and "valuable security" are defined in section 46.

127   A demand, which for the purposes of subsection 1(i) must be in writing, may be either express or implied. Where the prosecution seeks to prove an implied demand evidence of the circumstances in which the words were written would have to be adduced. In this respect, a distinction is drawn between a demand and a mere request.[62] However, a statement which is phrased in the language of a request can, when considered in the light of the circumstances in which it was made, amount to an implied demand.[63] Thus, in *R v Robinson*[64] the words "Remember, Sir, I am now only making an appeal to your benevolence" were held to amount to a demand. But, it is essential that the accused made a demand, however phrased, and an unsolicited offer by the prosecutor to pay the accused money falls outside the scope of the Act.

128   In essence, a menace is a threat of any action which is detrimental or unpleasant to the person to whom it is addressed.[65] Clearly it would include threats of violence to a person or property but it is not limited to such threats. Examples of threats which have been held to be menaces are threats to disclose the prosecutor's past sexual misdeeds,[66] to publish an attack on the prosecutor's business,[67] to place the prosecutor's name on a stop list operated by a trade association,[68] to withhold favourable evidence in a case in which the prosecutor is involved,[69] and to disclose the existence of a debt not honoured by the prosecutor.[70] It can be seen from those cases that were the threat to materialise the prosecutor's reputation or business

---

61   For a table of punishments see Ryan and Magee, *The Irish Criminal Process* (Cork, 1983) Appendix H.
62   *R v Studer* (1915) 11 Cr. App. R. 307.
63   *Ibid.*
64   (1796) 2 Leach 749.
65   *Thorne v Motor Trade Association* [1937] A.C. 797; *R v Tomlinson* [1895] 1 Q.B. 706.
66   *R v Tomlinson* [1895] 1 Q.B. 706.
67   *R v Boyle and Merchant* [1914] 3 K.B. 399.
68   *Thorne v Motor Trade Association* [1937] A.C. 797.
69   *R v Clear* [1968] 1 Q.B. 670.
70   *Norreys v Zeffert* [1939] 2 All E.R. 187.

would suffer, a consequence which few would disagree is grave. On the other hand, an innocuous or ineffective threat is not a menace. In *R v Clear*,[71] a prosecution under section 30, it was stated by the English Court of Appeal that a threat which would not influence a person of ordinary stability or courage is not a menace. It was on this basis that an offer to shopkeepers, for a contribution to charity, to provide a poster which would guarantee immunity from student rag activities was held not to be a menace.[72] It would seem that, for the purposes of subsection 1(i), the effect on the prosecutor of the threat is immaterial as long as it is capable of affecting an ordinary person. The offence is complete on uttering, the consequences of which are irrelevant.[73]

129   The accusations to which subsections 1(ii), 1(iii) and 2 refer are those of crimes listed in subsection 3. An accusation of a lesser offence, or of disreputable conduct which is not criminal, can be prosecuted under the general offence contained in subsection 1(i). The term "accuse" has an extensive meaning and is not confined to accusations made before a competent court; it includes an accusation before any third party.[74] The guilt or innocence of the person accused is irrelevant.[75]

130   Given the wide interpretation of "menace" it appears that many threats which are made in the course of everyday life are menaces. Examples are a threat to sue unless a claim is settled and a threat to leave employment unless a salary increase is granted. It is equally apparent that such threats are considered to be socially acceptable and should not be subject of punishment. To exclude such threats from the ambit of the criminal law it is provided that the accused must have acted without reasonable or probable cause. However, it should be noted that reasonable and probable cause is a defence to a charge under subsection 1 only; an accusation of crime is not capable of justification when its object is to enrich the accused. It has been held that what must be justified is the demand not the threat.[76] In short, the

71   [1968] 1 Q.B. 670; see also *R v Garwood* [1987] 1 All E.R. 1032; and paras 137-139 *infra*.

72   *R v Harry* [1974] Crim L.R. 32.

73   However, the case might be different where the accused is aware that the threat is innocuous; see paras 137-139 *infra*.

74   *R v Robinson* (1843) 2 M. & Rob. 14.

75   *R v Cracknell and Walker* (1866) 10 Cox C.C. 408.

76   *Thorne v Motor Trade Association* [1937] A.C. 797; *R v Hamilton* (1843) 1 Car. & K. 212.

crucial distinction is between justifiable demands and those which cannot be justified. Two issues which arise are what constitutes reasonable and probable cause and the relevance of the accused's belief. On both issues it is difficult to extract clear principles from the authorities.

131   In *R v Dymond*[77] the accused threatened to summons the prosecutor for indecent assault and to tell the townspeople of her allegation unless he paid her a sum of money. The trial judge refused to allow the prosecutor to be questioned about the alleged assault or to allow evidence to be adduced that the accused believed that she was entitled to make the demand. In upholding the conviction the English Court of Criminal Appeal stated that the question was one of fact for the jury to determine, but that an honest belief on the part of the accused did not constitute reasonable and probable cause. *Dymond* was followed in *R v Denyer*[78] where the accused, who threatened to place the prosecutor's name on the stop list operated by a trade association unless the association were paid a "fine", was held to have acted without justification. The court stated that there was no connection between the accused's right to place the prosecutor's name on the stop list and a right to demand money.[79]

132   Disapproval of *Denyer* was expressed in two civil cases, both of which concerned the same issue, namely a threat to place the plaintiff's name on a stop list unless he paid the association a sum of money. In *Hardie and Lane Ltd v Chilton*[80] the English Court of Appeal held that the plaintiffs could not recover the money paid by them. It was held that if there was no evidence of absence of reasonable and probable cause the case should be withdrawn from the jury. That question was considered to be distinct from that of honest belief on the part of the accused.[81] If an accused has a right to do a particular thing it cannot be unlawful for him to threaten to do it unless certain conditions are met, assuming of course that fulfilment of those conditions is not in itself unlawful. The case was equated with the settlement of a dispute which involves no criminality.[82] A further analogy drawn was that of a landowner who offers not to build on his

77   [1920] 2 K.B. 260.
78   [1926] 2 K.B. 258.
79   *Ibid.*, 268.
80   [1928] 2 K.B. 306.
81   *Ibid.*, 322.
82   *Ibid.*, 315-316, 317, 328.

land on condition that his neighbour pays a certain sum.[83] In that event the landowner is merely exercising a legal right which is vested in him. Scrutton LJ considered that the most obvious justification would be the existence on the part of the accused of a legal right to do the thing threatened.[84] The same conclusion was reached by the House of Lords in *Thorne v Motor Trade Association*.[85] Although the threat was a demand with menaces, the defendants were justified as it was made in the furtherance of their lawful business interests. However, Lord Atkin's speech was phrased in more cautious terms than the judgments in *Hardie and Lane*. He stated that the accused would have to be acting in the furtherance of some legitimate interest other than the acquisition of money and that the demand must be made *bona fide*. That qualification might refer to the particular legitimate interest in question, which was the right of a trade association to take action to protect the interests of its members. But the possibility is left open that the exercise of a right in some circumstances might fall short of reasonable and probable cause. The task for the courts will be to identify and define the extent of the legitimate interests which constitute reasonable and probable cause. For example, it might be that the courts would impose different limits on the right of trade unions to protect the interests of their members than those which are imposed on trade associations. The categorisation which the question will involve is, in essence, one of policy which is potentially fraught with political controversy.

133   The issue of the accused's belief in respect of the existence of reasonable and probable cause is still open. It has been noted that in *R v Dymond*[86] it was held that the accused's belief in this regard was irrelevant, but it is submitted that that is not the last word on the matter. In *Thorne* Lord Atkin questioned the correctness of that decision and considered some of the language used in the judgment to be incautious. In particular, he thought that a belief in the existence of facts which, if true, would furnish a reasonable and probable cause would be a defence.[87] This is no more than an application of the general defence of mistake of fact. Given modern developments in the law, that defence should be subjectively tested and it would be

---

83   *Ibid.*, 316.
84   *Ibid.*, 319
85   [1937] A.C. 797.
86   [1920] 2 K.B. 260.
87   [1937] A.C. 797, 809.

sufficient to show an honest, though not necessarily reasonable belief, on the part of the accused.[88] However, the belief would have to be as to circumstances which if they existed would in fact justify the accused's conduct. In other words, unlike the position under section 30,[89] claim of right would not be a defence to a charge brought under subsection 1. Stealing or an intent to steal is not an element of the offences contained in that subsection. However, intent to defraud is an ingredient of the offences contained in subsection 2 and, in principle, claim of right should be a defence. The apparent anomaly which thus arises, where claim of right is a defence to some of the offences under the section but not others, is the product of the manner in which the various offences are defined.

134   In *Hardie and Lane Ltd v Chilton* Scrutton LJ stated that subsection 4 was not very intelligible.[90] This was based on the view that as some of the provisions penalise the accusation of a crime it could hardly be immaterial whether the threats are of accusation.[91] However, it is submitted that what the subsection means is that the identity of the person who will bring about the threatened consequences — whether they be of violence, injury or accusation — is immaterial. This ensures that a threat of conduct by someone other than the accused falls within the section. Thus, the extortionist, who offers protection and suggests that "his boys" would be "disappointed" were the offer not accepted, is guilty just as if he threatened to effect the unpleasant consequence himself.

Section 30

[DEMANDING WITH MENACES, WITH INTENT TO STEAL]

30. Every person who with menaces or by force demands of any person anything capable of being stolen with intent to steal the same shall be guilty of felony and on conviction thereof liable to penal servitude for any term not exceeding five years.

---

88 See *R v Morgan* [1976] A.C. 182; *R v Gladstone Williams* (1984) 78 Cr. App. R. 276; more generally, see *The People (DPP) v Murray* [1976] I.R. 360.

89 See paras 139-141 *infra*.

90 [1928] 2 K.B. 306, 321.

91 *Ibid.*

135   The ingredients of the offence contained in section 30 differ from those of the offence in section 29(1)(i) in three major respects. The first is that demands are not confined to those contained in letters. Thus, for the purposes of the section, a demand can be made orally, in writing or by conduct.

136   The second difference is that the accused must have made a demand with menaces, whereas under the earlier section what is required is the uttering of a letter which demands with menaces. Receipt of the demand by the prosecutor is not necessary to complete that offence. However, it has yet to be decided whether receipt is required to complete the offence under section 30. In *R v Treacy*[92] the question was whether the appellant, who posted a letter in England received by the prosecutrix in West Germany, was guilty of blackmail under section 21 of the English Theft Act 1968.[93] By a majority of three-to-two, the House of Lords held that the appellant made the demand when he posted the letter and that the English courts accordingly had jurisdiction to try the case. Lord Hodson took the view that under the 1916 Act a demand could be made without its being received.[94] That was based on the decision of the English Court of Criminal Appeal in *R v Moran*[95] to the effect that there cannot be an attempt to demand. In Lord Hodson's opinion *Moran*, which he accepted as being generally correct, was intelligible only on the basis that a demand can be made without receipt; otherwise a person would be guilty of an attempt when he posted the letter.[96] However, the reasoning in *Moran* is unconvincing and the decision has been the subject of criticism.[97] Lord Diplock was content to state that "ordinary literate men and women" would conclude that a demand can be made without receipt.[98] It is submitted that *Treacy* should not

92   [1971] A.C. 537.
93   For the purposes of the case the crucial element was the making of an "unwarranted demand with menaces". The Act does not contain a provision similar to s. 29(1)(i) of the Larceny Act 1916. The appellant's conduct clearly would have amounted to an "uttering" within the meaning of that section.
94   [1971] A.C. 537, 557 (Lord Guest concurring)
95   (1952) 36 Cr. App. R. 10.
96   [1971] A.C. 537, 558.
97   See Edwards, (1952) 15 M.L.R. 346; Smith, [1961] Crim. L.R. 445; Russell, *Crime* (12th. ed., London, 1964) p. 878.
98   [1971] A.C. 537, 565. Lord Diplock based his approach principally on the question of jurisdiction and the presumption that statutory offences do not have extra-territorial effect.

be followed in this jurisdiction. Unlike the Theft Act 1968 the Larceny Act 1916 employs two phrases, namely "utters" and "demands". It must be assumed that the legislature had different meanings in mind when it employed those terms and to hold that a demand need not be received would be to confuse it with an uttering. Moreover, the decision in *Treacy* was narrow and the interpretation of "demand" was arrived at in an almost perfunctory manner.[99]

137   The meaning of menace has been considered in connection with section 29.[1] It has been established that a threat which would not influence a person of ordinary fortitude is not a menace.[2] Although that approach has been liberally interpreted, the question of the effect of the threat on the prosecutor has not been conclusively determined. In this context two cases arise: the first is where the threat would have affected a person of ordinary fortitude but did not affect the prosecutor; and the second is where the threat would not have affected an ordinary person but did affect the prosecutor.

138   It is conceivable that a threat which would affect the hypothetical ordinary person would not affect the particular person to whom it is directed. The latter might either be a person of remarkable fortitude or be aware of additional facts which make the threat innocuous. In *R v Clear*[3] the appellant addressed a threat to the managing director of the company by which he was employed. It would appear that the latter had no personal interest in the company and that he did not perceive any injury to the company should the threat materialise.[4] Despite that, the conviction was upheld. On that basis it would seem that the actual effect of the menace is immaterial as long as it is capable of operating on the mind of an ordinary person. However, there is a degree of confusion in the judgment between what constitutes a menace and the required intent to steal. Innocuous conduct was said to negative the intent to steal.[5] It was also stated that the circumstances which rendered the threat innocuous did not have a bearing on the appellant's state of mind, but that had he been aware

99 Lord Hodson, in particular, was influenced by the fact that the appellant's conduct would have been an offence under the 1916 Act and considered that it was not the intention of Parliament to create a new "loophole".
1   See para. 128 *supra*.
2   *R v Clear* [1968] 1 Q.B. 670; *R v Harry* [1974] Crim. L.R. 32.
3   [1968] 1 Q.B. 670.
4   However, he was sufficiently influenced to inform the police of the threats made by the accused.
5   [1968] 1 Q.B. 670, 679.

of them the case might have been different.[6] Despite the confusion, it is arguable that *Clear* is consistent with the gist of the offence which is that the accused demanded with menaces, not that the prosecutor was menaced. However, that depends on a definition of "menace" which ignores the ineffectiveness of the threat. It is debatable whether that is to be preferred to one which requires that the prosecutor be influenced by the threat. The question will have to be considered in the light of the object of the offence which, it is submitted, is to punish an accused for the making of an extortionist demand rather than one which he believes will have a contemplated effect.

139   The converse case is that of a prosecutor who is unusually timid and is affected by, what is for the ordinary person, an innocuous threat. In most cases the accused's defence would be based on an absence of intent to steal; if he was unaware of the prosecutor's peculiar disposition it would be difficult to infer intent from the threat. But a case might arise where the accused is familiar with the prosecutor's timidity and where intent to steal can be inferred. *Clear* suggests that the accused in that case would not be guilty. Thus, a potentially paradoxical position arises. The accused would be guilty where the threat is capable of influencing an ordinary person even though it did not influence the prosecutor but not guilty where a normally innocuous threat influenced the prosecutor. Given its object, it seems strange that the offence can, in some circumstances, be committed where the prosecutor is not intimidated, yet not be committed in other circumstances where the prosecutor is intimidated. Older authority to the effect that the demand must overbear the will of the prosecutor[7] was rejected in *Clear*. However, what the latter decided was that it is not necessary to prove that the prosecutor was threatened if the threat was capable of influencing an ordinary person. It does not follow that the older cases are not applicable where the prosecutor is in fact influenced by an otherwise innocuous threat. A possible reconciliation of the older cases with *Clear* is that actual fear on the part of the prosecutor is a sufficient, but not a necessary, condition to establish guilt, where the accused acts with the required intent. This, in effect, is the conclusion reached in *R v Garwood*[8] where it was held that the existence of a menace is

6   *Ibid.*, 680.
7   *R v Walton and Ogden* (1863) Le. & Ca. 288; see also *R v Collister and Warhurst* (1955) 39 Cr. App. R. 100.
8   [1987] 1 All E.R. 1032.

proved either where it is shown that the threat would have affected a person of ordinary stability although it did not affect the prosecutor *or* where the threat affected the prosecutor even though it would not have affected a person of ordinary stability. A problem with that decision is that, while *Clear* was cited in support of the first proposition, no authority was cited for the second nor was any conflict between the two forms of menace appreciated.

140   It is submitted that, apart from its unconvincing reasoning, *Garwood* should not be followed as it is an attempt to reconcile the irreconcilable; either a menace is a threat which actually operates on the mind of the prosecutor or it is one which is capable of operating on the mind of an ordinary person. It is inconsistent to say that the effect of the threat on the prosecutor is irrelevant in some cases yet relevant in others. To accommodate both within the definition of menace is a case of having one's cake and eating it and, it is submitted, a choice will face the Irish courts. If *Clear* is accepted the test will be whether the threat was capable of influencing an ordinary person regardless of its effect on the prosecutor. If *Clear* is rejected the attention will focus on the actual effect of the threat on the prosecutor. In this respect it is worth observing that, although the point was not expressed in the judgment, it is likely that *Clear* was influenced by the view, based on *R v Moran*,[9] that one could not be guilty of an attempt to demand with menaces. Thus, the only basis on which the appellant's conduct could be punished was that the full offence was committed. However, given the reservations which have been expressed about *Moran*,[10] it is open to the Irish courts to conclude that an attempt can be committed. This would allow the courts to hold that to constitute a menace the threat must have affected the prosecutor whilst ensuring that an accused could be convicted of an attempt where he committed a sufficiently proximate act which falls short of operating on the mind of the prosecutor.[11]

141   The third difference between the two offences lies in the intent required. Intent may be inferred from the fact that the threat was of such a nature as to affect an ordinary person.[12] It would seem that if

9   (1952) 36 Cr. App. R. 10.
10   See para. 136, note 97 *supra*.
11   An analogy can be drawn with the case of a false pretence which does not operate on the mind of the prosecutor; see *R v Hensler* (1870) 11 Cox C.C. 570 where the prosecutor was not deceived by the representations the accused was held guilty of an attempt as he had done all in his power to deceive.
12   *R v Clear* [1968] 1 Q.B. 670, 679.

the accused is aware that the prosecutor in fact would not be influenced by the threat intent is negatived.[13] As the intent required is an intent to steal regard must be had to the definition in section 1. Thus, in *R v Bernhard*[14] it was held that the existence of a claim of right was a defence as it negatived the element of fraud inherent in stealing.[15] In that case the accused threatened to disclose the prosecutor's former relationship with her unless he honoured a void contract to pay her certain sums of money. Moreover, it would appear that the claim of right would be a defence even though the accused did not believe that he is justified in using those means to enforce the claim.[16]

Section 31

[THREATENING TO PUBLISH, WITH INTENT TO EXTORT]

31. Every person who with intent —

(a) to extort any valuable thing from any person, or

(b) to induce any person to confer or procure for any person any appointment or office of profit or trust,

> *(1) publishes or threatens to publish any libel upon any other person (whether living or dead); or*

> *(2) directly or indirectly threatens to print or publish, or directly or indirectly proposes to abstain from or offers to prevent the printing or publishing of any matter or thing touching any other person (whether living or dead);*

shall be guilty of a misdemeanour and on conviction thereof liable to imprisonment, with or without hard labour, for any term not exceeding two years.

142   Section 31 re-enacts section 3 of the Libel Act 1843. It should be noted that, unlike section 29(1)(i), it does not contain an express requirement that there be an absence of reasonable and probable

13 *Ibid.*, 680.
14 [1938] 2 K.B. 264.
15 See para. 24 *supra*.
16 See *R v Skivington* [1968] 1 Q.B. 166.

cause. Were the section to be construed literally that omission would make the offence one of strict liability. Given the relatively light punishment which the offence attracts and its connection with libel the courts might adopt a strict interpretation.[17] On the other hand, what scant authority there is on the matter suggests that the existence of a reasonable and probable cause will absolve the accused. In *Thorne v Motor Trade Association* Lord Atkin, in one passage, equated sections 29(1)(i) and 31.[18] However, he made no further reference to section 31 in his speech. In *Burden v Harris*[19] the plaintiff, who won a bet from the defendant bookmaker, threatened to report him to Tattersalls Committee if he did not agree to pay. In an action to recover the agreed payment it was contended that the plaintiff's conduct amounted to an offence under section 31. This was rejected by Lawrence J who accepted that the decision in *Hyams v Stuart King*[20] was of general application to blackmail. In the latter case Farwell LJ exhibited a reluctance to describe as blackmail the use by a person of the ordinary means allowed by society to recover a dishonoured bet.[21] Despite the vagueness of the term "ordinary means allowed by society" the likely effect of these decisions is to imply a defence of reasonable and probable cause into the section. However, the omission of express words to that effect might be held to impose a burden of proof on the accused.[22] It should be noted that offences under section 31 are excluded from the power of arrest contained in section 41(1).

---

17 Libels were one of the few categories of offences which at common law attracted strict liability. For a recent instance see *R v Lemon and Gay News* [1979] A.C. 617; see generally *Toppin v Marcus* [1908] 2 I.R. 423; *McAdam v Dublin United Tramway Co Ltd* [1929] I.R. 327; Smith and Hogan, *Criminal Law* (London, 1983) pp. 87-108.

18 [1937] A.C. 797, 805.

19 [1937] 4 All E.R. 559.

20 [1908] 2 K.B. 696.

21 *Ibid.*, 726.

22 See *Sherras v De Rutzen* [1895] 1 Q.B. 918.

Section 32

[FALSE PRETENCES]

32. Every person who by any false pretence —

(1) with intent to defraud, obtains from any other person any chattel, money, or valuable security, or causes or procures any money to be paid, or any chattel or valuable security to be delivered to himself or to any other person for the use or benefit or on account of himself or any other person; or

(2) with intent to defraud or injure any other person, fraudulently causes or induces any other person —

(a) to execute, make, accept, endorse, or destroy the whole or any part of any valuable security; or

(b) to write, impress, or affix his name or the name of any other person, or the seal of any body corporate or society, upon any paper or parchment in order that the same may be afterwards made or converted into, or used or dealt with as, a valuable security;

shall be guilty of a misdemeanour and on conviction thereof liable to penal servitude for any term not exceeding five years.

143 Section 32 contains the offence of obtaining by false pretences. The offence applies to the obtaining of chattels, money and valuable securities, the latter being defined in section 46 (1). The essence of the offence is that the accused made a false representation of present fact, with intent to defraud, and thereby induced the owner to part with the property. The owner of the property must have intended to pass both possession and title to the property. Thus, a confidence trickster who induces a person to exchange goods on the false representation that he is their owner, is guilty of obtaining by false pretences; he is not guilty of larceny as the representee intended to pass property in the goods. On the other hand, if he induces the person to deliver the goods by pretending to be the owner's employee larceny by a trick is committed as the representee intends to pass possession only.[23] It is this factor which distinguishes the offence from larceny

23 *R v Sutton* [1966] 1 W.L.R. 236; see also *R v Caslin* [1961] 1 W.L.R. 59; *Anderson v Ryan* [1967] I.R. 34. The distinction between obtaining by false pretences and larceny by a trick has been considered in several civil cases

by a trick.

144   It is essential that the property was obtained and the offence is not committed where the accused merely retained property which had been given to him earlier.[24] Moreover, it must be proven that the property was obtained by means of the false pretence alleged.[25] It would be a good defence to show that the owner handed over the property regardless of the accused's representation. Likewise, it must be established that the representee believed the representation or at least that it operated on his mind.[26] If he did not believe it the offence is not complete, although the accused might be guilty of an attempt.[27]

145   The indictment must specify the pretence alleged and it is that pretence which must be shown to be false.[28] It is not sufficient to negative a different pretence and any variation between the pretence alleged and that proved is fatal.[29] In *The People (Attorney General) v Gilmore and Cunningham*[30] it was alleged that the accused entered a greyhound, called "Red Jack", in a race under the name "Funny Fish". The Supreme Court held that the charge was that one particular dog was substituted for another specified dog. Thus, it had to be proved that the dog concerned was "Red Jack" and not "Funny Fish". It was not sufficient to prove that there was a substitution of

where the plaintiff has been induced to part with goods by a confidence trickster. If the contract is void the offence is larceny by a trick, whereas if the contract is voidable the offence committed is obtaining by false pretences; see *Whitehorn Brothers v Davison* [1911] K.B. 463. In *Cundy v Lindsay* (1878) 3 App. Cas. 459 the rogue would have been guilty of larceny by a trick. The distinction is relevant where the trickster induces an owner to part with goods on credit terms. If it is a credit sale the offence would be obtaining by false pretences, and if it is a hire-purchase transaction the offence would be larceny by a trick. See also paras 49 and 50 *supra*.

24   *The People (Attorney General) v Singer* (1961) 1 Frewen 214.
25   *R v Kelleher* (1877) 2 L.R. Ir. 11.
26   *R v Sullivan* (1945) 30 Cr. App. R. 132.
27   *R v Hensler* (1870) 11 Cox C.C. 570.
28   *R v Kelleher* (1877) 2 L.R. Ir. 11; *The People (Attorney General) v Gilmore and Cunningham* (1950) 85 I.L.T.R. 99; *The People (Attorney General) v Thompson* (1960) 1 Frewen 201. In *White v The Queen* (1876) I.R. 10 C.L. 523 an indictment for conspiracy "by false pretences to defraud of large sums of money all such persons as should apply to or negotiate with [the accused] for a loan of money" was held to be bad for vagueness. In the course of its decision the Court of Queen's Bench stated that the mere averment of overt acts is not sufficient, and the alleged false pretences must be stated.
29   *Ibid.*
30   (1950) 85 I.L.T.R. 99.

dogs or that the dog run was not that which it was supposed to be. That would be to establish a pretence different from that alleged in the indictment.

146   The false pretence must be one of existing fact and not one as to the future. In general, statements of opinion and promises as to future conduct cannot amount to false pretences.[31] The pretence may consist of a statement or of conduct or of a combination of the two. In *R v Murphy*[32] the accused, who had ordered goods, sent half-notes by way of payment. At the time of sending she did not have the corresponding halves. It was argued on the accused's behalf that her conduct amounted merely to a promise to pay for the goods. The Court for Crown Cases Reserved rejected that argument and accepted the prosecution's argument that her conduct was an intimation that she was in possession of the corresponding halves and that the transaction was a ready made one. In *R v Dent*[33] the English Court of Criminal Appeal considered promises as to future conduct. The accused, a pest destructor, entered into contracts with farmers. He obtained payment in advance but subsequently did not perform. The alleged false pretences were that he was *bona fide* entering into the contracts and that he intended to perform them. The Court held that the promises made by the accused were not false pretences for the purposes of the criminal law. Such promises in themselves could not amount to false pretences. The Court acknowledged that a promise as to future conduct might be coupled with an allegation of existing fact, which if untrue would amount to a false pretence. Thus, there was an implied assertion that the accused was a pest destructor and that he had the means to do the work for which he had contracted. If the prosecution had negatived those assertions the Court implied that the offence would have been proven. In *R v Jones*[34] the accused, who entered into contracts to decorate premises, obtained advance payments to purchase materials. It appeared that he did not intend to honour the contracts. His conviction of fraudulent conversion was quashed, on the grounds that the persons who handed over the money intended property in it to pass. Lord Goddard CJ suggested that there was evidence to support a conviction of larceny by a trick, and said that the case was similar to that of a welshing bookmaker. However, it has

31   *R v Bryan* (1857) Dears. & B. 265.
32   (1876) I.R. 10 C.L. 508.
33   [1955] 2 Q.B. 590.
34   (1948) 33 Cr. App. R. 11.

been held that the welshing bookmaker is guilty of larceny by a trick because the owner of the money does not intend to part with property in the money.[35] If the persons who paid the accused to purchase the materials intended to part with property in the money then the offence is false pretences and not larceny by trick.

147   The presentation of a note or coin amounts to an assertion that it is genuine and an accused who presents false currency is guilty of the offence.[36] With regard to cheques it has been held that the drawer makes a number of representations: that he has an account in the bank on which the cheque is drawn; that he has authority to draw on the account for the amount of the cheque; and that the cheque is a valid order.[37] Unless otherwise indicated it must be assumed that the cheque will be presented for payment immediately.[38] In the case of a post-dated cheque the representation is that the cheque will be met on the appropriate date. A problem might arise where an accused draws a cheque on Friday night, knowing that his account is out of funds but believing that he will have sufficient funds on Monday morning. Such a cheque could be considered to be equivalent to a post-dated cheque and the accused would not be held to have made a false pretence.[39] In *The People (Attorney General) v Skelly*[40] the accused was given a post-dated cheque by a third party. When he became aware that the cheque was to be cancelled he cashed it with the prosecutor three days prior to its date. His conviction was quashed by the Court of Criminal Appeal as the prosecutor was a holder in due course of the cheque, whereas it had been assumed for the purposes of the prosecution that the cheque was worthless. The presentation of a credit card was held in *R v Lambie*[41] to amount to a representation that the accused has authority to make a contract with a shop on behalf of his bank.

148   Subsection 2 is aimed at documents which impose a liability on another to pay money or perform an obligation on behalf of the accused or someone else. If, on the other hand, the document imposes a liability on the accused only the offence is not established. In *R v*

35 *R v Buckmaster* (1887) 20 Q.B.D. 182.
36 *The People (Attorney General) v Finkel and Levine* (1951) 1 Frewen 123.
37 *The People (Attorney General) v Thompson* (1960) 1 Frewen 201.
38 *The People (DPP) v Shanahan* (1978) 1 Frewen 417.
39 The accused in that case would also have a defence of lack of intent to defraud; see para. 150 *infra*.
40 [1935] I.R. 604.
41 [1982] A.C. 449.

Thornton[42] the accused, who was overdrawn, executed a bill of exchange in favour of his bank. The bill was in respect of goods which he falsely represented to be his. In consequence, a bank employee was induced to sign the bill as witness under section 8 of the Bills of Sale Act (1878) Amendment Act 1882. He was held not to be guilty of an offence under subsection 2 as the bill did not impose liability on anyone other than himself.[43]

149   To secure a conviction under either subsection it must be established that the accused acted with intent to defraud. In general, the jury should be directed as to this point, although an express direction might not be required.[44] However, the omission to direct the jury expressly has been said to be "a perilous course",[45] particularly where the defence is based on lack of intent. It has been stated that unless the intent is obvious the jury should be directed that it is an essential element.[46] Intent to defraud may be inferred from the facts of the case.[47] Where money is obtained by a false pretence there is a *prima facie* case of intent to defraud.[48] In *The People (Attorney General) v Sullivan*[49] the Supreme Court held that the submission of false claims for payment was *prima facie* evidence of intent to defraud. In *The People (DPP) v Shanahan*[50] it was held that the fact that the accused's account was out of funds when the cheque was drawn coupled with his false explanation of the matter to the police was *prima facie* evidence of intent.

150   Although proof of the accused's knowledge of the falsity of the representation supports a *prima facie* case of intent to defraud, such proof is not always sufficient. The ultimate question is whether the accused intended to defraud and not merely whether he knew that the representation was false.[51] The accused can rebut such a case of intent

42 [1964] 2 Q.B. 177.
43 But the accused was held guilty of obtaining credit by false pretences contrary to s. 13(1) of the Debtors Act 1869 on the ground that by forebearing to enforce the existing debt the bank extended credit to him.
44 *The People (Attorney General) v Thompson* (1960) 1 Frewen 201; *The People (Attorney General) v Bristow* (1961) 1 Frewen 249.
45 *The People (Attorney General) v Bristow* (1961) 1 Frewen 249.
46 *The People (Attorney General) v Thompson* (1960) 1 Frewen 201.
47 *The People (Attorney General) v Bristow* (1961) 1 Frewen 249.
48 *The People (Attorney General) v Thompson* (1960) 1 Frewen 201.
49 [1964] I.R. 169.
50 (1978) 1 Frewen 417.
51 *The People (Attorney General) v Thompson* (1960) 1 Frewen 201.

by showing that he believed that payment would be made or that he was ignorant of the falsity of his representation. In *The People (Attorney General) v Thompson*[52] the accused paid for goods with a post-dated cheque. He had hoped to arrange for a quick resale of the goods and to have sufficient funds to meet the cheque. He subsequently lodged a second cheque in his account in order to meet the first cheque. The drawer of the second cheque stopped payment and, accordingly, when the first cheque was presented the account was out of funds. The Court of Criminal Appeal, in quashing his conviction, held that his belief that the account would be in funds by the date of the cheque negatived intent to defraud. It was not sufficient for the prosecution to establish that he did not have authority to draw on his account when the cheque was written. In the similar case of *The People (DPP) v Shanahan*[53] the Court of Criminal Appeal stated that the onus is on the prosecution to show that, at the time the cheque was issued, the accused was aware that it was unlikely to be met out of the account on which it was drawn. The accused's knowledge that the account is out of funds is evidence on which a jury can find an intent to defraud, but it may be rebutted by evidence that the accused expected the account to be in funds when the cheque would be presented for payment.

151   It should be noted that section 10 of the Criminal Justice Act 1951 contains an offence of obtaining by false pretences which, in essence, is similar to the offence under this section. Section 13(1) of the Debtors (Ireland) Act 1872 contains the offence of obtaining credit by false pretences.

Section 33

[RECEIVING]

33.—(1) Every person who receives any property knowing the same to have been stolen or obtained in any way whatsoever under circumstances which amount to felony or misdemeanour, shall be guilty of an offence of the like degree (whether felony or misdemeanour) and on conviction thereof liable —

    (a) in the case of felony, to penal servitude for any term not

52   (1960) 1 Frewen 201.
53   (1978) 1 Frewen 417.

exceeding fourteen years;

(b) in the case of misdemeanour, to penal servitude for any term not exceeding seven years;

(c) in either case, if a male under the age of sixteen years, to be once privately whipped in addition to any punishment to which he may by law be liable.

(2) Every person who receives any mail bag, or any postal packet, or any chattel, or money, or valuable security, the stealing, or taking, or embezzling, or secreting whereof amounts to a felony under the Post Office Act, 1908, or this Act, knowing the same to have been so feloniously stolen, taken, embezzled, or secreted, and to have been sent or to have been intended to be sent by post, shall be guilty of felony and on conviction thereof liable to the same punishment as if he had stolen, taken, embezzled, or secreted the same.

(3) Every such person may be indicted and convicted, whether the principal offender has or has not been previously convicted, or is or is not amenable to justice.

(4) Every person who, without lawful excuse, knowing the same to have been stolen or obtained in any way whatsoever under such circumstances that if the act had been committed in the United Kingdom the person committing it would have been guilty of felony or misdemeanour, receives or has in his possession any property so stolen or obtained outside the United Kingdom, shall be guilty of an offence of the like degree (whether felony or misdemeanour) and on conviction thereof liable to penal servitude for any term not exceeding seven years.

152   Section 33 creates a series of offences which prohibit the receipt by a person of property which has been wrongfully acquired by another. The acquisition of the property by that other amounts to larceny or some other offence. The receiving of the property is an offence of the same degree as the principal offence. A further offence of unlawful possession of property which was wrongfully acquired outside the jurisdiction is created by subsection 4.[53a]

153   The case law in this jurisdiction deals exclusively with receiving stolen property, but there is nothing to suggest that the principles do not apply to the other forms of receiving. The essential feature of

53a See the Law Reform Commission's *Report on Receiving Stolen Property*, (LRC 23 — 1987).

receiving is a receipt by the accused of property which, to his or her knowledge, was stolen by someone else. Receiving has been stated to require proof of three ingredients: that the property was stolen by someone other than the accused; that the property was in the accused's possession; and that at the time of receipt the accused knew the property was stolen.[54] It is not uncommon to charge an accused with both larceny and receiving of the same property, but they are charged in the alternative and it is inconsistent to convict of both.[55] Often the evidence points to both offences, but the crucial difference is that, in a case of receiving, the prosecution must prove that the property was stolen by someone other than the accused. Thus, simply to establish that the accused was found in possession of stolen property is insufficient to secure a conviction of receiving, proof of a theft by someone else being necessary.[56] This point must be brought to the attention of the jury, although a specific direction to that effect is not required if it is made otherwise clear.[57] In the absence of evidence that someone other than the accused stole the property the only possible conviction open is larceny. Where the evidence points either way it is a matter for the jury to determine the offence of which the accused is guilty.[58]

154   To secure a conviction of receiving it must be established that the property was stolen and that it was that property which the accused received;[59] it is not an offence to receive the proceeds of the stolen property.[60] Equally, it is not an offence to receive property which has reverted to possession of the owner or someone authorised to acquire

54 *R v McMahon* (1875) 13 Cox C.C. 275.

55 *The People (Attorney General) v Byrne* (1966) 1 Frewen 303.

56 *R v McMahon* (1875) 13 Cox C.C. 275; *The People (Attorney General) v Carney and Mulcahy* [1955] I.R. 324.

57 *The People (Attorney General) v Duggan* [1958] I.R. 116.

58 *R v McMahon* (1875) 13 Cox C.C. 275; *The People (Attorney General) v Carney and Mulcahy* [1955] I.R. 324.

59 *Attorney General v Conway* (1925) 60 I.L.T.R. 41 (conviction quashed due to lack of evidence that the goods found in the accused's possession were the stolen goods). Where goods are taken by a child who is *doli incapax* no offence is committed and, consequently, a receiver is not guilty of receiving; see *Walters v Lunt* [1951] 2 All E.R. 645.

60 *Attorney General v Farnan* (1933) 67 I.L.T.R. 208. However, there is English authority to the contrary based on the definition of "property" in s.46(1) which includes property into which it is converted; see *D'Andrea v Woods* [1953] 1 W.L.R. 1307; *R v Froggett* [1966] 1 Q.B. 152.

it on his behalf.[61] Thus, if the police recover stolen goods, but allow the thief's plan to proceed in order to apprehend the receiver, receipt by the latter is not an offence. Moreover, if the indictment alleges that the property was stolen by a particular person, a failure to establish that fact will be fatal.[62] Receipt of the property is established by proof that it was in the accused's possession at some stage. In this context the normal principles governing possession apply; the accused must be shown to have had some knowledge of the existence of the goods.[63] However, it is not necessary to prove that the accused had actual possession of the property, constructive possession being sufficient.[64] In *The People (Attorney General) v Lawless*[65] the Court of Criminal Appeal, in the course of discussing constructive possession, expressed its approval of the statement in Archbold that:[66]

> The actual manual possession or touch of the goods by the prisoner, however, is not necessary to the completion of the offence of receiving; it is sufficient if they are in the actual possession of a person over whom the accused has a control, so that they would be forthcoming if he ordered it.

Thus, an accused who arranges for the stolen property to be deposited with a friend, to keep for him until he can collect it, is guilty of receiving. The property is in the constructive possession of the accused as he can order its delivery at any time. Likewise, property held by one on behalf of others is in their constructive possession.[67]

155   It must be established that the accused knew that the property was wrongfully acquired. It is sufficient to prove that the accused knew the goods to have been acquired by an offence of the same degree, that is by a felony or a misdemeanour, as the case may be.[68] But if the

---

61 *R v Villensky* [1892] 2 Q.B. 597.
62 *R v Connolly and Hughes* (1838) 1 Cr. & D. (AB. Not. Co.) 280.
63 *The People (Attorney General) v Nugent and Byrne* (1964) 98 I.L.T.R. 139; *The People (Attorney General) v Carney and Mulcahy* [1955] I.R. 324; see also *Minister for Posts and Telegraphs v Campbell* [1966] I.R. 69 for a general discussion of the law governing possession.
64 *The People (Attorney General) v Kelly and Robinson* (1953) 1 Frewen 147.
65 (1968) 1 Frewen 338.
66 36th. ed., para. 2096.
67 *The People (Attorney General) v Kelly and Robinson* (1953) 1 Frewen 147.
68 *DPP v Nieser* [1958] 3 All E.R. 662.

accused believes the goods to have been stolen, when in fact they have been obtained by false pretences, receipt of them is not an offence.[69] It is crucial that the knowledge existed at the time at which the property was received.[70] A specific direction to that effect might not be necessary if the jury's attention is drawn to it in some other way. If, however, they are led to believe that knowledge at any time whilst the accused was in possession is sufficient the direction will be held to be bad.[71] The Court of Criminal Appeal considered the test to be applied in *The People (Attorney General) v Berber and Levy*.[72] The Court stated the general proposition that the prosecution bears the responsibility of proving guilty knowledge beyond reasonable doubt. The question is whether the accused knew that the property was stolen when he received it. The test is not one of commercial prudence or reasonableness. A person might be so imprudent that he did not know that the property was stolen, where, had he not been imprudent, he would have known it was stolen. Such imprudence, rather than proving guilty knowledge, negates it. A test of ordinary prudence would make imprudence a badge of fraud. A reasonable mind might be satisfied that a transaction is imprudent or incautious without its being criminal. However, although the Court did not consider the point, it may be speculated that imprudence or unreasonableness is evidence of guilty knowledge. A person who accepts property which he suspects is stolen might be held to have guilty knowledge. In that event the prosecution would seek to rely on the accused's subjective recklessness, and wilful blindness would be considered to be equivalent to actual knowledge.[73]

156   Frequently the prosecution relies on proof that the accused was found in possession of the property shortly after it was stolen, coupled with the accused's failure to explain that possession adequately. The doctrine of recent possession was considered by the Court of Criminal Appeal in *The People (Attorney General) v Oglesby*.[74] The Court stated that the doctrine is merely an explanation of inferences which may reasonably be drawn if the accused gives no explanation of his possession of the property. It does not, however, place an onus on the

69   *Ibid.*
70   *The People (Attorney General) v Lillis* [1958] I.R. 188.
71   *Ibid.*
72   [1944] I.R. 405.
73   See *The People (DPP) v Murray* [1976] I.R. 360 for a general discussion of the law on knowledge.
74   [1966] I.R. 163.

accused to provide an explanation or to prove that the possession was innocent, and it is a misdirection to suggest otherwise.[75] The doctrine is, therefore, a convenient expression of the proposition that an accused who does not explain the possession of recently stolen property runs the risk of being found guilty.[76] In other words, the jury may infer guilt from proof of recent possession.

157   Recent possession can be evidence either of larceny or of receiving. In general, it is for the jury to determine which offence, if either, the accused has committed.[77] They must, of course, be satisfied that someone other than the accused stole the property before convicting of receiving.[78] However, if the possession is so close in point of time to the theft, as to exclude the possibility of anyone else having had possession of the property, the case should go to the jury on a charge of larceny only.[79] What is "recent" is a matter of fact which is related to the circumstances of the case, and, in particular, to the nature of the property.[80] For instance, a period which is considered to be recent in the case of rare antiques is not necessarily recent in respect of a television set.

158   If the accused provides a reasonable explanation of his recent possession the prosecution should, but is not obliged to, give rebutting evidence.[81] The ultimate question is whether the prosecution has proved its case beyond reasonable doubt. That question is distinct from the truth, probability or reasonableness of the accused's explanation.[82] The issue is not whether the jury believes the accused's explanation but whether the accused is proven to have had guilty

75 *Ibid.*; *The People (Attorney General) v Melody* (1967) 1 Frewen 319.

76 In *DPP v Nieser* [1958] 3 All E.R. 662, 669 Diplock J suggested that recent possession without proof of additional facts is evidence that the accused believed the goods to be stolen but not that they were otherwise wrongfully acquired.

77 In *The Minister for Industry and Commerce v Pim* [1966] I.R. 155, 161 Davitt P suggested, *obiter*, that where it is clear that the accused committed one of the offences, but the jury is uncertain which is the true explanation of the possession, they are not bound to acquit but can convict of the offence which they consider is more appropriate.

78 See para. 153, notes 56 and 57 *supra*.

79 *The People (Attorney General) v Carney and Mulcahy* [1955] I.R. 324.

80 *R v McMahon* (1875) 13 Cox C.C. 275; *The People (Attorney General) v Finnegan* [1933] I.R. 292.

81 *The People (Attorney General) v Finnegan* [1933] I.R. 292.

82 *The People (Attorney General) v Berber and Levy* [1944] I.R. 405; *The People (Attorney General) v Lillis* [1958] I.R. 188.

knowledge. That explanation, at best, is evidence one way or the other. A direction to the jury to convict if they disbelieve the accused's story is bad if it suggests that conviction is the necessary consequence of that finding.[83] Likewise, a reference to the accused's failure to give an explanation amounts to a misdirection if it conveys to the jury the impression that the prosecution's case is thereby strengthened.[84]

159   The effect of subsection 4 is to create two distinct offences, namely receiving property which was stolen or otherwise unlawfully acquired outside the jurisdiction, and being in possession of property so acquired. The property received must have been taken outside the jurisdiction in circumstances which, if taken within the jurisdiction, would amount to an offence.[85] The offence is committed if that property is received within the jurisdiction.[86] However, a receiving outside the jurisdiction does not, in itself, constitute an offence.[87] The separate offence of being in possession of property which was stolen outside the jurisdiction would be committed, if the possession was within the territory of the State.

160   The interpretation of the phrase "the United Kingdom" was considered by the Supreme Court in *The People (Attorney General) v Ruttledge*.[88] The problem was that those words were not expressly adapted by the relevant adaptation legislation. That legislation adapted "Ireland" to "Saorstát Éireann"[89] and subsequently to "Ireland", in the sense of the Republic of Ireland.[90] The Court split the phrase "United Kingdom" into its component parts, namely Great Britain and Ireland. The result is that that phrase is to be read as meaning Great Britain and the Republic of Ireland. Thus, if the property is stolen in Northern Ireland the subsection will apply, but not if it is stolen in Great Britain. In the latter case the stealing does not occur outside "the United Kingdom". In *The State (Gilsenan) v McMorrow*[91] the Supreme Court confirmed its earlier decision. The

---

83 *The People (Attorney General) v Oglesby* [1966] I.R. 163; *The People (Attorney General) v Melody* (1967) 1 Frewen 319.

84 *The People (Attorney General) v Duggan* [1958] I.R. 116.

85 See *R v Smith* [1962] 2 Q.B. 317.

86 *The People (Attorney General) v Finnegan* [1933] I.R. 292.

87 *Attorney General v McGinley* [1945] I.R. 373.

88 [1978] I.R. 376. The case was decided in 1947 but was not reported until 1978.

89 Adaptation of Enactments Act 1922, s. 3.

90 Constitution (Consequential Provisions) Act 1937, s. 2.

91 [1978] I.R. 360.

Court also held that the expression "Northern Ireland", which was used in the indictment, was not vague or ambiguous. It felt that the phrase clearly refers to that area of the island over which the State does not exercise jurisdiction and that judicial notice should be taken of that meaning.

161   Subsection 3, which establishes that a person may be charged with and convicted of receiving notwithstanding that the thief has not been apprehended, governs cases where the property was stolen within the jurisdiction.[92] Where, however, the thief testifies on behalf of the prosecution the trial judge must warn the jury of the dangers of convicting on his uncorroborated evidence. It is for the trial judge to determine whether the witness is an accomplice, and the warning must be absolute, not conditional.[93] The trial judge should also specify those counts the evidence for which is uncorroborated.[94] In *The People (Attorney General) v Shaw*[95] the evidence of a third party that he bought the property from the accused shortly after the theft, in the absence of an explanation by the accused, was held to corroborate the thief's evidence.

Section 34

[CORRUPTLY TAKING A REWARD]

34. Every person who corruptly takes any money or reward, directly or indirectly, under pretence or upon account of helping any person to recover any property which has, under circumstances which amount to felony or misdemeanour, been stolen or obtained in any way whatsoever, or received, shall (unless he has used all due diligence to cause the offender to be brought to trial for the same) be guilty of felony and on conviction thereof liable to penal servitude for any term not exceeding seven years, and, if a male under the age of sixteen years, to be once privately whipped in addition to any other punishment to which he may by law be liable.

92 *R v Smith* [1962] 2 Q.B. 317.
93 *The People (Attorney General) v Carney and Mulcahy* [1955] I.R. 324.
94 *The People (Attorney General) v Shaw* [1960] I.R. 168.
95 *Ibid.*

162 To come within the terms of the section it must be established that the property which the accused proposed to recover was stolen or otherwise criminally acquired. It does not apply where the property was acquired innocently or even tortiously. The reward is taken by the accused either on the pretence of recovering the property or on account of recovery. It is not necessary to prove a connection between the accused and the person who unlawfully acquired the property.[96] It is sufficient that the accused took the money without honestly meaning to make efforts to bring the wrongdoer to justice.[97] Thus, a "broker" who undertakes to recover property on a "no questions asked" basis would be guilty of an offence. In *R v Pascoe*[98] the accused, who accepted money in order to purchase stolen property from the thieves without intending to bring them to justice, was held to be guilty of the equivalent offence under an earlier statute.[99] In *R v O'Donnell*[1] it was held that it was not essential that the reward be paid before the return of the property. If the accused is aware of a prior agreement to pay and delivers the property accordingly the payment is taken "on account of helping . . . to recover".[2] It should be noted that section 5(3) provides for the taking of rewards to recover stolen dogs. Moreover, section 102 of the Larceny Act 1861 creates a penal action where a person advertises, or publishes or prints an advertisment, for the return of stolen property on a "no questions asked" basis.

Section 35

[ACCESSORIES AND ABETTORS]

35. Every person who knowingly and wilfully aids, abets, counsels, procures or commands the commission of an offence punishable under this Act shall be liable to be dealt with, indicted, tried and punished as a principal offender.

96 *R v King* (1845) 1 Cox C.C. 36.
97 *Ibid.*
98 (1849) 1 Den. 456.
99 7 & 8 Geo. 4 c. 29 s. 58.
1 (1857) 7 Cox C.C. 337.
2 *Ibid.*, 342.

Section 36

163   Section 36 was repealed by section 19 of the Married Women's Status Act 1957. Section 9 of that Act deals with the prosecution of one spouse in respect of an offence against the property of the other. A prosecution may not be initiated if the spouses are living together or, if separated, in respect of conduct while they were cohabiting. However, proceedings may be taken if the property was wrongfully appropriated when a spouse was leaving or deserting the other.

Section 37

[PUNISHMENTS]

37.—(1) Every person who commits the offence of simple larceny after having been previously convicted of felony shall be liable to penal servitude for any term not exceeding ten years.

(2) Every person who commits the offence of simple larceny, or any offence made punishable like simple larceny, after having been previously convicted—

(a) of any indictable misdemeanour punishable under this Act; or

(b) twice summarily of any offence punishable under section six of the Summary Jurisdiction (Ireland) Act, 1851, or under the Larceny Act, 1861, or under the Malicious Damage Act, 1861, or under this Act (whether each of the convictions has been in respect of an offence of the same description or not, and whether such convictions, or either of them, have been before or after the passing of this Act);

shall be liable to penal servitude for any term not exceeding seven years.

(3) In every case in this section before mentioned the offender, if a male under the age of sixteen years, shall be liable to be once privately whipped in addition to any other punishment to which he may by law be liable.

(4) Where a sentence of penal servitude may be imposed on conviction of an offence against this Act, the court may instead thereof impose a sentence of imprisonment, with or without hard labour, for

not more than two years.

(5)—(a) On conviction of a misdemeanour punishable under this Act the court, instead of or in addition to any other punishment which may be lawfully imposed, may fine the offender.

(b) On conviction of a felony punishable under this Act the court, in addition to imposing a sentence of penal servitude or imprisonment, may require the offender to enter into his own recognizances, with or without sureties, for keeping the peace and being of good behaviour.

(c) On conviction of a misdemeanour punishable under this Act the court, instead of or in addition to any other punishment which may lawfully be imposed for the offence, may require the offender to enter into his own recognizances, with or without sureties, for keeping the peace and being of good behaviour.

(d) Provided that a person shall not be imprisoned for more than one year for not finding sureties.

(6) Where a sentence of whipping may be imposed under this Act—

(a) in the case of an offender whose age does not exceed sixteen years, the number of strokes at such whipping shall not exceed twenty-five and the instrument used shall be a birch-rod;

(b) in the case of any other offender, the number of strokes at such whipping shall not exceed fifty;

(c) in each case the court in its sentence shall specify the number of strokes to be inflicted and the instrument to be used;

(d) such whipping shall not take place after the expiration of six months from the passing of the sentence;

(e) such whipping to be inflicted on any person sentenced to penal servitude shall be inflicted on him before he is removed to a convict prison with a view to his undergoing his sentence of penal servitude.

Section 38

[JURISDICTION OF QUARTER SESSIONS]

38.—(1) A court of quarter sessions —

(a) notwithstanding anything in the Quarter Sessions Act, 1842, shall in England have jurisdiction to try an indictment for burglary;

(b) shall not have jurisdiction to try an indictment for any offence against sections twenty, twenty-one, and twenty-two of this Act.

(2) A justice of the peace in England when committing for trial a person charged with burglary shall commit him for trial before a court of assize unless, owing to the absence of any circumstances which make the case a grave or difficult one, he thinks it expedient in the interest of justice to commit him for trial before a court of quarter sessions; and the Assizes Relief Act, 1889, shall apply.

164   The provisions of section 38, which have not been repealed, are, quite obviously, otiose. Offences under the Act are triable summarily where the District Justice is of the view that the offence is minor in nature and the accused consents to summary trial.[3]

Section 39

[VENUE]

39.—(1) A person charged with any offence against this Act may be proceeded against, indicted, tried, and punished in any county or place in which he was apprehended or is in custody as if the offence had been committed in that county or place; and for all purposes incidental to or consequential on the prosecution, trial, or punishment of the offence, it shall be deemed to have been committed in that county or place.

(2) Every person who steals or otherwise feloniously takes any property in any one part of the United Kingdom may be dealt with, indicted, tried, and punished in any other part of the United Kingdom where he has the property in his possession in the same manner as if he had actually stolen or taken it in that part.

(3) Every person who receives in any one part of the United Kingdom any property stolen or otherwise feloniously taken in any other part of the United Kingdom may be dealt with, indicted, tried, and punished in that part of the United Kingdom where he so receives the property in the same manner as if it had been originally stolen or taken in that part.

3   Criminal Justice Act 1951, s. 2 and Criminal Procedure Act 1967, s. 19(2).

165   The provisions of subsection 1 have been superceded by those of section 25(3) of the Courts (Supplemental Provisions) Act 1961 which allow an accused to be tried in the circuit in which the alleged offence was committed or in which the accused was arrested or resides.[4]

166   It must be assumed that subsections 2 and 3 are redundant.[5] The phrase "United Kingdom" in those subsections refers to Great Britain and the Republic of Ireland.[6] That phrase has not been expressly adapted but the cumulative effect of adaptation legislation is to adapt "Ireland", which by implication is included in the "United Kingdom", to "Saorstát Éireann" and, subsequently, to "Ireland" in the sense of the Republic of Ireland; the remainder of the phrase, namely Great Britain, was left unaffected.[7] However, it does not follow that an Irish court would have jurisdiction to try an accused for an offence which has been committed in England. The purpose of the section when enacted was to deal with jurisdiction within the state — which at the time was the United Kingdom of Great Britain and Ireland — not to confer an extraterritorial jurisdiction on the courts. Such jurisdiction could not be assumed by implication from the failure expressly to adapt the words "United Kingdom". That conclusion is supported by the provisions of section 2(2) of the Constitution (Consequential Provisions) Act 1937 which preclude an implied extension of the area of application of laws through the adaptation of the phrase "Saorstát Éireann". The clear inference is that the adaptation process does not imply an extension of offences beyond the territorial limits of the State.[8]

---

4   For the transfer of trials to the Dublin Circuit see s. 31 of the Courts Act 1981. It should be noted that none of the offences in the Larceny Act are triable in the Central Criminal Court; see *Tormey v Ireland* [1985] I.L.R.M. 375.

5   In *R v McQuillan* [1923] 2 I.R. 93 the Court of Appeal for Northern Ireland held that the Northern Irish courts had jurisdiction to try a case of robbery which was committed in Co. Leitrim in October 1922; but the court stated that their decision was not applicable to offences committed after December 6, 1922.

6   *The People (Attorney General) v Ruttledge* [1978] I.R. 376; *The State (Gilsenan) v McMorrow* [1978] I.R. 360.

7   *Ibid.*; see s. 3 of the Adaptation of Enactments Act 1922 and s. 2 of the Constitution (Consequential Provisions) Act 1937.

8   It has been suggested that the section is no longer effective on the ground that references to the United Kingdom must be taken as references to the State; see Ryan and Magee *The Irish Criminal Process* (Cork, 1983) p. 26, note 4. But *Ruttledge* and *Gilsenan*, note 6 *supra*, have decided otherwise.

Section 40

[PROCEDURE]

40.—(1) On the trial of an indictment for obtaining or attempting to obtain any chattel, money, or valuable security by any false pretence, it shall not be necessary to prove an intent to defraud any particular person, but it shall be sufficient to prove that the person accused did the act charged with intent to defraud.

(2) An allegation in an indictment that money or banknotes have been embezzled or obtained by false pretences can, so far as regards the description of the property, be sustained by proof that the offender embezzled or obtained any piece of coin or any banknote or any portion of the value thereof, although such piece of coin or banknote may have been delivered to him in order that some part of the value thereof should be returned to any person and such part has been returned accordingly.

(3) In an indictment for feloniously receiving any property under this Act any number of persons who have at different times so received such property or any part thereof may be charged and tried together.

(4) If any person, who is a member of any co-partnership or is one of two or more beneficial owners of any property, steals or embezzles any such property of or belonging to such co- partnership or to such beneficial owners he shall be liable to be dealt with, tried, and punished as if he had not been or was not a member of such co-partnership or one of such beneficial owners.

(5) In Ireland the following provisions shall have effect with respect to indictments:—

(a) In an indictment for an offence against this Act with reference to any instrument, it shall be sufficient to describe such instrument by any name or designation by which it is usually known, or by its purport, without setting out any copy or facsimile thereof or otherwise describing it or its value:

(b) In an indictment for any offence of stealing under this Act, distinct acts of stealing, not exceeding three, which have been committed by the person accused against the same person within the space of six months, may be charged in separate counts of the same indictment and tried together:

(c) If on the trial of an indictment for stealing any property it *appears that the property alleged in such indictment to have been stolen at one time was take at different times, such separate takings may be tried together to a number not exceeding three, provided that not more than the space of six months elapsed between the first and the last of such takings:*

(d) In an indictment for any offence of embezzlement or of fraudulent application or disposition against this Act, distinct acts of embezzlement or of fraudulent application or disposition not exceeding three, which have been committed by him against the same person within the space of six months, may be charged in separate counts of the same indictment and tried together; and where such offence relates to any money or valuable security it shall not be necessary to specify any particular coin or valuable security; and such allegation shall be sustained whether the offender is proved to have embezzled or to have fraudulently applied or disposed of any amount, although the particular coin or valuable security of which such amount was composed is not proved, or whether he is proved to have embezzled or to have fraudulently applied or disposed of any valuable security which has been delivered to him in order that some part of the value thereof should be returned to any person and such part has been returned accordingly:

(e) In every case of stealing any chattel or fixture under section sixteen of this Act (relating to tenants and lodgers) it shall be lawful to prefer an indictment in the same form as if the offender were not a tenant or lodger:

(f) In an indictment for stealing any document of title to lands, it shall be sufficient to allege such document to be or to contain evidence of the title or of part of the title of the person or of someone of the persons having an interest, whether vested or contingent, legal or equitable, in the real estate to which the same relates, and to mention such real estate or some part thereof:

(g) In an indictment for an offence under this Act with respect to any will, codicil, or other testamentary document, record, or other legal document whatsoever, or anything made of metal fixed in any square or street, or in any place dedicated to public use or ornament, or in any burial-ground, it shall not be necessary to allege the same to be the property of any person:

(h) In an indictment under section sixteen of this Act it shall be

lawful to lay the property alleged to be stolen in the owner or person letting to hire:

(i) In an indictment for obtaining or attempting to obtain any chattel, money, or valuable security by any false pretence, it shall be sufficient to allege that the person accused did the act with intent to defraud, without alleging an intent to defraud any particular person and without alleging any ownership of the chattel, money, or valuable security:

(j) Charges of stealing any property and of feloniously receiving the same property or any part thereof may be included in separate counts of the same indictment and such counts may be tried together:

(k) Any person or persons charged in separate counts of the same indictment with stealing any property and with feloniously receiving the same property or any part thereof may severally be found guilty either of stealing or of receiving the said property or any part thereof.

167 In *R v Tizard*[9] it was held that subsection 3 is not confined to cases of successive receiving; once it is alleged that the property was stolen in the one transaction it is permissible to charge all alleged receivers in one indictment, whether they received from the thief or each other and whether the original thief is joined in the indictment or not.[10]

168 In *Attorney General v Reilly*[11] it was held that an indictment which charged more than three counts of fraudulent conversion was not bad despite the provisions of subsection 5(d). Rule 3 of the First Schedule to the Criminal Justice (Administration) Act 1924 provides for the joinder of multiple charges on an indictment and, to that extent, the provisions of this section are amended. The Rule does not limit the number of charges which may be included in an indictment, but section 6(3) of the same Act confers a discretion on the court to order separate trials where it is of the opinion that the accused may be prejudiced or embarrassed in his defence by reason of the multiplicity of charges.[12] Moreover, the Court of Criminal Appeal has noted a

9   [1962] 2 Q.B. 608.
10 See also s. 6 of the Accessories and Abettors Act 1861. S. 44(5) of this Act was said by the court to sanction in retrospect what s. 40(3) authorises in advance.
11 [1937] I.R. 118.
12 See *The People (DPP) v Wallace* (1982) 2 Frewen 125.

tendency towards an unnecessary proliferation of counts in indictments and the clear inference is that the right to include multiple charges in an indictment is not unfettered.[13]

Section 41

[ARREST WITHOUT WARRANT]

41.—(1) Any person found committing any offence punishable under this Act except an offence under section thirty-one may be immediately apprehended without a warrant by any person and forthwith taken, together with the property, if any, before a justice of the peace to be dealt with according to law.

(2) Any person to whom any property is offered to be sold, pawned, or delivered, if he has reasonable cause to suspect that any offence has been committed against this Act with respect to such property, shall, if in his power, apprehend and forthwith take before a justice of the peace the person offering the same, together with such property, to be dealt with according to law.

(3) Any constable or peace officer may take into custody without warrant any person whom he finds lying or loitering in any highway, yard, or other place during the night, and whom he has good cause to suspect of having committed or being about to commit any felony against this Act, and shall take such person as soon as reasonably may be before a justice of the peace to be dealt with according to law.

169 Section 41 contains a number of powers of arrest which supplement, but do not replace, the powers of arrest conferred at common law. The general principle adopted by Irish courts in the construction of statutory powers of arrest is one of strict interpretation; powers must be conferred expressly and the courts will not extend them by implication.[14] Subsection 1 contains a general power which is

---

13 *The People (Attorney General) v Coughlan* (1968) 1 Frewen 325, 331-2.
14 See generally *Barry v Midland Rly. Co.* (1867) I.R. 1 C.L. 130; *Forbes v Lloyd* (1876) I.R. 10 C.L. 552; *Fox v Great Southern Rly.* (1940) 75 I.L.T.R. 2; *The People (DPP) v Madden* [1977] I.R. 336; *The State (Hoey) v Garvey* [1978] I.R. 1; *The State (Walshe) v Maguire* [1979] I.R. 372.

conferred on all, whilst the powers in subsections 2 and 3 are confined to persons to whom property is offered for sale and Gardai, respectively. The power contained in subsection 3 may only be exercised at night, the extent of which is defined in section 46. References to justices of the peace have been replaced by District Justices[15] and Peace Commissioners.[16]

170   Under subsection 1 a person whom one "finds committing" an offence may be arrested "immediately" and brought before a District Justice "forthwith". In this respect, "immediately" means then and there and the arrest may not be postponed on the grounds of convenience; if an arrest on the spot is impossible the power may be exercised following a pursuit of the offender.[17] As the power is confined to those who are "found committing" an offence an arrest may not be made where the offender is discovered after the offence has been committed. However, the courts have been prepared to relax the strictness of that phrase by invoking a theory of continuing acts. In *Griffith v Taylor*[18] it was held that the taking of goods continues as long as their removal continues and, accordingly, a thief who is discovered as he escapes is found committing larceny. It would seem that the power is confined to the arrest of actual offenders and that it does not extend to those who are suspected of committing an offence. The subsection omits words to that effect and if it is to be interpreted strictly that omission cannot be altered by implication. On the other hand, there is a series of English cases in which the same phrase in other statutes has been held to include a power to arrest those who are reasonably suspected of being "found committing" the offence in respect of which the power is conferred.[19] However, it has been stated that the phrase must be construed in the context of the particular statute in which it appears without reference being made to other

---

15 See s. 6(1) of the Adaptation of Enactments Act 1922.

16 See s. 88 of the Courts of Justice Act, 1924. For brevity, references in the text to District Justice include, where appropriate, Peace Commissioners. However, doubt on the constitutionality of the role of Peace Commissioners was expressed by Walsh J in *The State (Lynch) v Ballagh* [1987] I.L.R.M. 65, 71-2.

17 *Griffith v Taylor* (1876) 2 C.P.D. 194.

18 (1876) 2 C.P.D. 194.

19 *Trebeck v Croudace* [1918] 1 K.B. 158; *Isaacs v Keech* [1925] 2 K.B. 354; *Barnard v Gorman* [1941] A.C. 378; *Wiltshire v Barrett* [1966] 1 Q.B. 312; *Walker v Lovell* [1975] 1 W.L.R. 1141; *Wills v Bowley* [1983] 1 A.C. 57.

statutes.[20] Were the question to arise in relation to subsection 1 the courts would be faced with a conflict between interpreting the provision strictly and an approach which modifies the strict wording of the provision.[21] It is submitted that the former approach is to be preferred as it is consistent with general principle.[22] Moreover, the English cases which adopted a modified meaning were principally concerned with summary offences relating to safety on the highway, in respect of which no general power of arrest existed.

171   A person who is arrested under subsections 1 or 2 must be brought "forthwith" before a District Justice. This can be contrasted with subsection 3 which provides that the person arrested under that subsection should be brought before a District Justice "as soon as reasonably may be". "Forthwith" means directly and it would be unlawful to bring the arrestee to a Garda station in the first instance. In *Walsh v Pender*[23] the power, in section 61 of the Malicious Damages Act 1861, to arrest and bring an offender "forthwith" before a District Justice was considered. It was held that that power did not entitle the defendant to bring the plaintiff to a Garda station. It follows that the Gardai would not be permitted to detain or interrogate a person arrested under subsections 1 or 2. The provision in subsection 3 that the arrestee be brought before a District Justice "as soon as reasonably may be" reflects the common law position. In this respect the reasonableness of the delay in bringing the arrestee before a District Justice will depend on the circumstances of the case and it would probably be permissable to detain him overnight.[24] Moreover, it would appear that whilst so detained the Gardai may interrogate the arrestee.[25]

---

20 *Barnard v Gorman* [1941] A.C. 378; *Wiltshire v Barrett* [1966] 1 Q.B. 312. Lord Diplock has suggested that the courts should take account of the legal characteristics of common law arrest when interpreting statutory powers; see *Walker v Lovell* [1975] 1 W.L.R. 1141, 1149-50.

21 The question is unlikely to arise in practice, as it is probable that reliance will be placed on the common law power to arrest for felony.

22 See cases cited in para. 169, note 14 *supra*.

23 (1927) 62 I.L.T.R. 8.

24 See *Dunne v Clinton* [1930] I.R. 360; *The People (DPP) v Walsh* [1980] I.R. 294.

25 See *The People (DPP) v McCann* (1981) 2 Frewen 57; *The People (DPP) v Quilligan* [1986] I.R. 495. On the latter case, see further McCutcheon, "Arrest, Investigate and Section 30" (1987) 9 D.U.L.U. (n.s.) 46.

Section 42

[SEARCH WARRANTS]

42.—(1) If it is made to appear by information on oath before a justice of the peace that there is reasonable cause to believe that any person has in his custody or possession or on his premises any property whatsoever, with respect to which any offence against this Act has been committed, the justice may grant a warrant to search for and seize the same.

(2)—(a) Any constable or peace officer may, if authorised in writing by a chief officer of police, enter any house, shop, warehouse, yard, or other premises, and search for and seize any property he believes to have been stolen, and, where any property is seized in pursuance of this section, the person on whose premises it was at the time of seizure or the person from whom it was taken shall, unless previously charged with receiving the same knowing it to have been stolen, be summoned before a court of summary jurisdiction to account for his possession of such property, and such court shall make such order respecting the disposal of such property and may award such costs as the justice of the case may require.

(b) It shall be lawful for any chief officer of police to give such authority as aforesaid—

(i) when the premises to be searched are or within the preceding twelve months have been in the occupation of any person who has been convicted of receiving stolen property or of harbouring thieves; or

(ii) when the premises to be searched are in the occupation of any person who has been convicted of any offence involving fraud or dishonesty and punishable with penal servitude or imprisonment.

(c) It shall not be necessary for such chief officer of police on giving such authority to specify any particular property, but he may give such authority if he has reason to believe generally that such premises are being made a receptacle for stolen goods.

172 The powers of search and seizure which are conferred by this section supplement those enjoyed at common law, the most important of which is the power of search which is incidental to a lawful

arrest.[26] References in the section to justices of the peace have been replaced by District Justices[27] and Peace Commissioners.[28]

173   At common law property which is reasonably believed to be stolen or to be unlawfully in the possession of an arrested person may be seized even though the arrest is made for another offence.[29] This, however, would appear to be superceded by section 9 of the Criminal Law Act 1976 which allows the seizure of "anything [believed] to be evidence of any offence or suspected offence". The only precondition to the valid exercise of section 9 is that the Gardai were exercising a power under the 1976 Act or any other search power.

174   The power conferred by subsection 2 on a "chief officer of police" to authorise searches is constitutionally suspect. That power is confined to permitting the search of premises occupied by certain categories of convicted persons. In this respect the provision does not hold all persons equally before the law and could amount to a violation of Article 40.1 of the Constitution. Moreover, the fact of the occupier's conviction is, in essence, substituted for reasonable suspicion that the premises contain stolen goods. This could be said to violate the concept of justice which is implicit in the Constitution and, in particular, the provision in Article 38.1 that trials be in due course of law.[30]

Section 43

[EVIDENCE]

43.—(1) Whenever any person is being proceeded against for receiving any property, knowing it to have been stolen, or for having in his possession stolen property, for the purpose of proving guilty knowledge there may be given in evidence at any stage of the

26 *Dillon v O'Brien and Davis* (1887) 20 L.R. Ir. 300; see also *Jennings v Quinn* [1968] I.R. 305.

27 See s. 6(1) of the Adaptation of Enactments Act 1922.

28 See s. 88 of the Courts of Justice Act 1924. In *Ryan v O'Callaghan*, High Court, unreported, 22 July 1987, Barr J held the power of a peace commissioner to issue a warrant under s. 42(1) to be constitutional.

29 *Jennings v Quinn* [1968] I.R. 305; see also *Chic Fashions (West Wales) Ltd v Jones* [1968] 2 Q.B. 299; *Frank Truman Export v Metropolitan Police Commissioner* [1977] Q.B. 952.

30 See *King v Attorney General* [1981] I.R. 233.

proceedings —

(a) the fact that other property stolen within the period of twelve months preceding the date of the offence charged was found or had been in his possession;

(b) the fact that within the five years preceding the date of the offence charged he was convicted of any offence involving fraud or dishonesty.

This last-mentioned fact may not be proved unless —

(i) seven days' notice in writing has been given to the offender that proof of such previous conviction is intended to be given;

(ii) evidence has been given that the property in respect of which the offender is being tried was found or had been in his possession.

(2) No person shall be liable to be convicted of any offence against sections six, seven subsection (1), twenty, twenty-one, and twenty-two of this Act upon any evidence whatever in respect of any act done by him, if at any time previously to his being charged with such offence he has first disclosed such act on oath, in consequence of any compulsory process of any court of law or equity in any action, suit, or proceeding which has been bona fide instituted by any person aggrieved.

(3) In any proceedings in respect of any offence against sections six, seven subsection (1), twenty, twenty-one, and twenty-two of this Act, a statement or admission made by any person in any compulsory examination or deposition before any court on the hearing of any matter in bankruptcy shall not be admissible in evidence against that person.

175   The provisions of subsection 1, which re-enact those of section 19 of the Prevention of Crimes Act 1871, are an exception to the general rule that evidence of the accused's previous convictions may not be adduced. The subsection allows for the admission of such evidence where the accused is charged with receiving, or being in possession, of stolen property. From the wording of the subsection it is plain that such evidence may not be adduced where the charge is of receiving, or being in possession of, property which has been otherwise wrongfully acquired.[31] The evidence may be adduced for the purpose of establishing guilty knowledge on the part of the accused. It should

31   Moreover, if a count is added charging larceny evidence may not be adduced under s. 43(1); see *R v Davies* [1953] 1 Q.B. 489.

be remembered that possession involves an element of knowledge[32] and, in this respect, the distinction between evidence of guilty knowledge and that of knowledge which establishes possession can be slight. In *R v List*[33] it was stated that the court has an overriding discretion to exclude evidence which is admissible under the subsection if its prejudicial effect would make it impossible for the jury to take a dispassionate view of the crucial facts of the case. That decision was approved by the English Court of Criminal Appeal in *R v Herron*.[34] In *R v Wilkins*,[35] a decision which involved the equivalent English provision,[36] the accused was charged on a number of counts, some of which concerned guilty knowledge and others in which possession was the crucial question. It was stated that in those circumstances the trial judge should exercise great care in deciding whether to admit the evidence and that if the evidence is admitted care should be taken to explain its relevance to the jury.

176   The constitutionality of subsection 1 must be called into question, as a result of the decision of the Supreme Court in *King v Attorney General*.[37] In that case certain of the provisions of section 4 of the Vagrancy Act 1824 were held to be unconstitutional. That section was amended by section 15 of the Prevention of Crimes Act 1871 to allow the required intent to commit a felony to be established on proof of the accused's known character. In effect, the prosecution was absolved of the necessity to adduce evidence of overt acts from which the intent could be inferred and that was held to violate the concept of justice which is implicit in the Constitution.[38] Both from the terms and general tenor of the judgments in *King* it appears that it is constitutionally impermissible to found a conviction on proof of the accused's previous convictions and, in this respect, subsection 1 suffers from the same defect as that of the impugned offence.

177   The effect of subsections 2 and 3 is to exclude evidence which would be otherwise admissible, being disclosed on a lawful examination in judicial proceedings.[39]

---

32   See paras 14 and 154, note 63 *supra*.
33   [1966] 1 W.L.R. 9.
34   [1967] 1 Q.B. 107.
35   [1975] 2 All E.R. 734.
36   S. 27(3) of the Theft Act 1968.
37   [1981] I.R. 233.
38   *Ibid.*, 242, 249, 256-7.
39   See *R v Scott* (1856) 7 Cox C.C. 164; *The State (McCarthy) v Lennon* [1936] I.R. 485; *R v Dawson* [1960] 1 W.L.R. 163.

Section 44

[VERDICT]

44.—(1) If on the trial of any indictment for robbery, it is proved that the defendant committed an assault with intent to rob, the jury may acquit the defendant of robbery and find him guilty of an assault with intent to rob, and thereupon he shall be liable to be punished accordingly.

(2) If on the trial of any indictment for any offence against section seventeen of this Act (relating to embezzlement) it is proved that the defendant stole the property in question, the jury may find him guilty of stealing, and thereupon he shall be liable to be punished accordingly; and on the trial of any indictment for stealing the jury may in like manner find the defendant guilty of embezzlement or of fraudulent application or disposition, as the case may be, and thereupon he shall be liable to be punished accordingly.

(3) If on the trial of any indictment for stealing it is proved that the defendant took any chattel, money, or valuable security in question in any such manner as would amount in law to obtaining it by false pretences, with intent to defraud, the jury may acquit the defendant of stealing and find him guilty of obtaining the chattel, money or valuable security by false pretences, and thereupon he shall be liable to be punished accordingly.

(4) If on the trial of any indictment for obtaining any chattel, money, or valuable security by false pretences it is proved that the defendant stole the property in question, he shall not by reason thereof be entitled to be acquitted of obtaining such property by false pretences.

(5) If on the trial of any two or more persons indicted for jointly receiving any property it is proved that one or more of such persons separately received any part of such property, the jury may convict upon such indictment such of the said persons as are proved to have received any part of such property.

178 The provisions of section 44 allow for the substitution of verdicts in certain cases. Thus, the combined effect of subsections 3 and 4 is to allow a jury to substitute a verdict of guilty of larceny in a trial for obtaining by false pretences and *vice versa*. Moreover, the trial judge may direct the jury to acquit of one charge and leave to them the

question of guilt of the substituted alternative.[40] It should be noted that an accused who is charged with an offence for which conviction of an alternative may be substituted is placed in jeopardy in respect of both offences. In *The People (Attorney General) v Heald*[41] the accused was convicted on a charge of fraudulent conversion and acquitted on one of larceny. On appeal it was held that her conduct, if culpable, amounted not to fraudulent conversion but to obtaining by false pretences.[42] However, as the accused was in peril of being convicted of that offence on the larceny charge a re-trial on a charge of false pretences was precluded.[43]

179   It has been held that the power to substitute verdicts is not vested in the Special Criminal Court, as section 44 created a substantive jurisdiction which is not a mere matter of practice and procedure.[44]

Section 45

[RESTITUTION]

45.—(1) If any person guilty of any such felony or misdemeanour as is mentioned in this Act, in stealing, taking, obtaining, extorting, embezzling, converting, or disposing of, or in knowingly receiving, any property, is prosecuted to conviction by or on behalf of the owner of such property, the property shall be restored to the owner or his representative.

(2) In every case in this section referred to the court before whom such offender is convicted shall have power to award from time to time writs of restitution for the said property or to order the restitution thereof in a summary manner:

Provided that where goods as defined in the Sale of Goods Act, 1893, have been obtained by fraud or other wrongful means not amounting to stealing, the property in such goods shall not re-vest in the person

40 *The People (Attorney General) v O'Brien* [1963] I.R. 65.
41 [1954] I.R. 58.
42 See para. 84 *supra.*
43 But an accused who is acquitted of obtaining by false pretences may be retried for conspiracy to defraud based on the same acts; see *Attorney General v Hurley and Woolfson* (1936) 71 I.L.T.R. 29.
44 *The People (DPP) v Rice* [1979] I.R.15.

who was the owner of the goods or his personal representative, by reason only of the conviction of the offender:

And provided that nothing in this section shall apply to the case of—

> *(a) any valuable security which has been in good faith paid or discharged by some person or body corporate liable to the payment thereof, or, being a negotiable instrument, has been in good faith taken or received by transfer or delivery by some person or body corporate for a just and valuable consideration without any notice or without any reasonable cause to suspect that the same had been stolen;*
>
> *(b) Any offence against sections twenty, twenty-one, and twenty-two of this Act.*

(3) On the restitution of any stolen property if it appears to the court by the evidence that the offender has sold the stolen property to any person, and that such person has had no knowledge that the same was stolen, and that any moneys have been taken from the offender on his apprehension, the court may, on the application of such purchaser, order that out of such moneys a sum not exceeding the amount of the proceeds of such sale be delivered to the said purchaser.

180   Section 45 allows the court to order the restitution of property where the offender is successfully prosecuted and where the circumstances of the wrongful acquisition are such as to preclude a vesting of title in the offender. Title remains with the owner where the property is stolen, robbed, embezzled, extorted or received, but not when it is obtained by false pretences.[45] The proviso in subsection 2 reflects the provisions of section 24(2) of the Sale of Goods Act 1893. By virtue of the definition of ''property'' in section 46(1) an order may be made in respect of property into which the stolen property has been converted. Thus, where an accused pays the proceeds of a theft into a bank account an order may be made in respect of the account; the chose in action which the account represents is property into which the stolen property was converted.[46]

181   Title to goods purchased *bona fide* at market overt vests in the purchaser.[47] However, if the thief is convicted title automatically

45   See *Anderson v Ryan* [1967] I.R. 34; and see paras 49, 50 and 143 *supra*.

46   *Barclays Bank v Milne* [1963] 1 W.L.R. 1241.

47   S. 22 of the Sale of Goods Act 1893.

revests in the owner[48] and restitution may be ordered.[49] The innocent purchaser is left to pursue a civil remedy in that case. However, subsection 3 allows the court to order that he be compensated out of any money which the offender has in his possession at the time of his apprehension.

182   An order under this section may not be made in respect of negotiable instruments which are held by *bona fide* holders for value nor in respect of property which has been fraudulently converted.

Section 46

[INTERPRETATION]

46.—(1) In this Act, unless the context otherwise requires,—
The expression "chief officer of police" means —

> *(a) In the city of London, the Commissioner of City Police;*
> *(b) In the Metropolitan Police District, the Commissioner of Police of the Metropolis;*
> *(c) In any other police district in England, the officer having the chief command of the police in such police district;*
> *(d) In the police district of Dublin Metropolis, either of the commissioners of police for the said district;*
> *(e) In any other police district in Ireland, the sub- inspector of the Royal Irish Constabulary;*
> *and shall include any person authorised by such said chief officer of police to act in his behalf:*

The expression "document of title to goods" includes any bill of lading, India warrant, dock warrant, warehouse-keeper's certificate, warrant or order for the delivery or transfer of any goods or valuable thing, bought or sold note, or any other document used in the ordinary course of business as proof of the possession or control of goods, or authorising or purporting to authorise, either by endorsement or by delivery, the possessor of such document to transfer or receive any goods thereby represented or therein mentioned or referred to:

The expression "document of title to lands" includes any deed, map, roll, register, paper, or parchment, written or printed, or partly

---

48   S. 24(1) of the Sale of Goods Act 1893.
49   See *The Queen v Horan* (1872) I.R. 6 C.L. 293.

written and partly printed, being or containing evidence of the title, or any part of the title, to any real estate or to any interest in or out of any real estate:

The expressions "mail," "mail bag," "officer of the Post Office," "postal packet," "post office," and "in course of transmission by post," shall have the same meanings in this Act as in the Post Office Act, 1908:

The expression "night" means the interval between nine o'clock in the evening and six o'clock in the morning of the next succeeding day:

The expression "property" includes any description of real and personal property, money, debts, and legacies, and all deeds and instruments relating to or evidencing the title or right to any property, or giving a right to recover or receive any money or goods, and also includes not only such property as has been originally in the possession or under the control of any person, but also any property into or for which the same has been converted or exchanged, and anything acquired by such conversion or exchange, whether immediately or otherwise:

The expression "trustee" means a trustee on some express trust created by some deed, will, or instrument in writing, and includes the heir or personal representative of any such trustee, and any other person upon or to whom the duty of such trust shall have devolved or come, and also an executor and administrator, and an official receiver, assignee, liquidator, or other like officer acting under any present or future Act relating to joint stock companies or bankruptcy:

The expression "valuable security" includes any writing entitling or evidencing the title of any person to any share or interest in any public stock, annuity, fund, or debt of any part of His Majesty's Dominions, or of any foreign state, or in any stock, annuity, fund, or debt of any body corporate, company, or society, whether within or without His Majesty's Dominions, or to any deposit in any bank, and also includes any scrip, debenture, bill, note, warrant, order, or other security for payment of money, or any accountable receipt, release, or discharge, or any receipt or other instrument evidencing the payment of money, or the delivery of any chattel personal, and any document of title to lands or goods as hereinbefore defined.

(2) The expression "dwelling-house" does not include a building although within the same curtilage with any dwelling-house and occupied therewith unless there is a communication between such

building and dwelling-house, either immediate or by means of a covered and enclosed passage leading from one to the other.

(3) References in this Act to any Act in force at the commencement of this Act shall be held to include a reference to that Act as amended, extended, or applied by any other Act.

183 The expression "chief officer of police" means, in Dublin, the Commissioner or Assistant Commissioner of the Garda Síochána and, in any other police district, the Superintendent of the Garda Síochána for that area.[50]

184 The expressions contained in the fourth paragraph of subsection 1 are defined in section 89 of the Post Office Act 1908, duly modified to take account of the establishment of An Post.[51] In *Hood v Smith*[52] a test letter placed in the post with the object of apprehending a dishonest postal employee was held to be a postal packet in the course of transmission by post.

185 By virtue of sections 46 and 51(4) of the Currency Act 1927 legal tender notes and consolidated bank notes are respectively deemed to be valuable securities.

Section 47

[SAVINGS]

47.—(1) Where, by virtue of some other Act, an offence against this Act subjects the offender to any forfeiture or disqualification, or to any penalty other than penal servitude or fine, the liability of the offender to punishment under this Act shall be in addition to and not in substitution for his liability under such other Act.

(2) Where an offence against this Act is by any other Act, whether passed before or after the commencement of this Act, made punishable on summary conviction, proceedings may be taken either under such other Act or under this Act: Provided that where such an offence was at the commencement of this Act punishable only on summary conviction, it shall remain only so punishable.

50 See Sandes, *Criminal Practice, Procedure and Evidence in Eire* (Dublin, 1951) p. 50.
51 See s. 8(1), Sch. 4 Postal and Telecommunications Services Act 1983.
52 (1933) 30 Cox C.C. 82.

Section 48

[REPEALS]

48.—(1) *The enactments specified in the Schedule to this Act are hereby repealed as to England and Ireland to the extent specified in the third column thereof.*

(2) For the purposes of the First Schedule to the Summary Jurisdiction Act, 1879, the first subsection of the thirty-third section of this Act shall be substituted for the ninety-first and ninety-fifth sections of the Larceny Act, 1861.

Section 49

[EXTENT]

49. *This Act shall not extend to Scotland, except as hereinbefore otherwise expressly provided.*

Section 50

[SHORT TITLE AND COMMENCEMENT]

50. *This Act may be cited as the Larceny Act, 1916, and shall come into operation on the first day of January nineteen hundred and seventeen.*

Some Thoughts on Reform

186   At this stage a consideration of the law of larceny turns to the question of its reform. Since the passing of the Larceny Act 1916 the major reform has been the alteration of the offences of robbery, burglary and aggravated burglary by the Criminal Law (Jurisdiction) Act 1976.[53] The purpose of that reform was to ensure correspondence between those offences in Northern Ireland and Ireland which, it was presumed, would facilitate the operation of the extraterritorial scheme established by the Act.[54] An attempt, in the Larceny (Amendment) Bill 1985, to amend the provisions of section 28, on possession of implements for stealing, and to replace the offence of receiving, in section 33, with one of handling stolen goods failed.[55] However, the question of a general reform of the law of larceny has not been considered since the enactment of the Act.

187   Any suggestion of reform presupposes that the law is in some way deficient and fails to meet its social objectives. With regard to larceny the traditional criticism is that it is founded on an unduly technical base, namely the concept of possession, which leads to artificial, and uncertain, distinctions between discrete offences. Thus, the distinction between larceny by a trick and obtaining by false pretences is seen as being one without a difference. Why should the accused's liability depend on the, often undisclosed, intention of the prosecutor in respect of the goods?[56] In both cases the accused acquires goods through some fraudulent deceit and his conduct is of equal moral repugnance and social harm. Underlying that criticism is the view that the law fails in what is considered to be its primary objective of protecting property by penalising its dishonest acquisition. The belief is that the technical nature of the law and its uncertain divisions frustrate that objective and facilitate the acquittal of dishonest persons who merit conviction. The tempting conclusion is that a less complex and better defined law would be more effective in achieving that objective.

53   See paras 91-117 *supra*.
54   See *Law Enforcement Commission Report* Prl. 3832, p 22.
55   See *Dail Debates*, Vol. 363, Cols 255, 782-809, 1557-1586 and 1795-1828; The replacement of receiving with an offence of handling stolen goods has been recommended recently; see the Law Reform Commission's *Report on Receiving Stolen Property* (LRC 23 — 1987).
56   See paras 49-50 and 143 *supra*.

188   However, to state that a rational criminal code should protect property by penalising dishonest acquisition over- simplifies matters. No code penalises all dishonesty which disrupts property ownership and the initial question is one of identifying those acquisitions which merit a criminal sanction, those which ought to be resolved by the civil law and those which should be considered to be lawful. It is not difficult to conceive of cases of dishonesty, such as unfair price fixing, making of excessive profits and abuse of market position, which typically do not, nor would not, fall within the scope of the criminal code of a western society. Though disreputable, and indeed deserving of condemnation, those practices are considered to be part of a capitalist society and although they might require regulation they do not merit punishment. In this respect, the question is one of social perception or, indeed, of imagery. Thieves, embezzlers and confidence-tricksters are seen to be criminals whilst overchargers, gazumpers and market monopolists are not. In this context it is useful to remember that the law of larceny emerged not to protect property, which was considered to fall within the province of the civil law, but principally to preserve the peace. In the course of its development it underwent a metamorphosis during the eighteenth century which altered its objectives and the punishment of dishonesty became the principal concern.[57] The history of the law since then has been one of attempts to bring more instances of dishonesty within its scope. Its product is the division of the law on dishonest appropriations into the four discrete offences of larceny, embezzlement, fraudulent conversion and obtaining by false pretences.

189   Thus, the law on dishonest appropriations and the categories which it employs are principally the result of historical accident. But that in itself is reason neither for its preservation nor its reform. The issue is whether the law makes adequate provision for those acquisitions which are considered to merit punishment. That leads back to the initial question, alluded to already, of identifying those acquisitions which merit punishment. At its most fundamental it can be argued that to reform the law of a capitalist society is pointless as to do so is merely to reiterate or reinforce its unequal distribution of wealth; property is theft and theft law, being property law, is inherently unjust. Thus, on this view what ought to be reformed is not the law but society. However, a more cautious version of that ideological perspective can accommodate legal reform. The question then is

57   See Fletcher, "The Metamorphosis of Larceny" (1976) 89 Harv. L.R. 469.

whether certain conduct which is tolerated in a capitalist society, such as unjust enrichment at the expense of the economically vulnerable through dishonest and anti-social business practices, ought to penalised. Those, however, are political matters in the resolution of which lawyers do not enjoy a moral monopoly. That is not to suggest that lawyers are absolved of their political responsibilities, much less that law reform can be apolitical; the point is that the lawyer's view on the matter deserves no greater attention than that of anyone else. However, once the political parameters are set, within which reform is to take place, the lawyer's expertise allows comment on the practicality of that reform. Given contemporary political reality the question is thus narrowed to whether the law adequately deals with the punishment of those whose dishonesty offends the social consensus of a capitalist society. In other words, are those whose conduct matches the image of criminality adopted by that society brought within the scope of the criminal law. In that respect attention will focus on the ease with which the law can be administered.

190   The technical nature of this area of the law is considered to obscure its divisions and lead to difficulties in its application. The arbitrary boundaries between the various offences can result in the acquittal of those whose appropriations ought to be condemned as being criminal. For instance, it is not always certain whether an accused should be charged with larceny by a trick or obtaining by false pretences and the current state of the law might be seen to allow wrongdoers to benefit from prosecutorial uncertainty. To an extent these difficulties have been ameliorated by the provisions in section 44 which allow for the substitution of verdicts.[58] A related question is whether the current state of the law leaves unpunished forms of conduct which ought to be punished. To judge from experience as reflected in the law reports the legal system has not been burdened with difficulties in this regard. The paucity of reported decisions on this area suggests that we are relatively content with the law and that there is little need for major reform. This can be contrasted with the English experience prior to the enactment of the Theft Act 1968 which shows the law there to have been in a state of tension. In particular, reference can be made to the doctrine of trespassory taking[59] and the postponement of the acquisition of possession until the accused has become aware of

58   See paras 178-179 *supra*.
59   See paras 17 and 38 *supra*.

the goods in his custody.[60] The latter is instructive as the question has been considered in both jurisdictions and has resulted in different interpretations of the ambiguous decision in *R v Ashwell*.[61] The English approach resulted in a series of decisions on the point which are difficult, if not impossible, to reconcile.[62] Those difficulties were largely avoided in Ireland as a result of the decision in *R v Hehir*[63] which had the effect of leaving unpunished certain forms of conduct which probably would have attracted criminal sanction in England.[64]

191 The differences between the law in the two jurisdictions possibly reflect different cultural perceptions on dishonesty and its punishment. The English decisions manifest a greater concern than is evident in Irish cases to punish dishonesty at the expense of doctrinal consistency, a development which was universally condemned by commentators. Two principal problems were discerned. One was that the law was being stretched to accommodate the punishment of more forms of dishonesty. The second was that, despite judicial creativity, some forms of dishonesty were left unpunished. In effect both problems point to a perceived underlying inflexibility in the law which failed to meet contemporary demands made of it. In consequence, a new departure was marked with the enactment of the Theft Act 1968 which abandoned larceny and replaced it with a new scheme. Dishonest appropriations are now provided for by the offence of theft and a series of offences which involve obtaining by deception. The offence of theft replaced the old rules on possession and substituted the concept of dishonest appropriation which embraces a wider range of conduct than "taking and carrying away".[65] The definition of deception is broader than false pretences; it covers representations, by words or conduct, of fact, law or the present intentions of the accused.[66] The other major changes made by

60 See paras 20-21 *supra*.
61 (1885) 16 Q.B.D. 190
62 See paras 20-21 and 52 *supra*.
63 [1895] 2 I.R. 709.
64 See para. 19 *supra*.
65 S. 1 of the Theft Act 1968 provides: "A person is guilty of theft if he dishonestly appropriates property belonging to another with the intention of permanently depriving the other of it; . . .". The expressions "dishonestly" and "appropriates" are amplified in ss. 2 and 3 respectively.
66 S. 15(4) of the Theft Act 1968 defines "deception" as being ". . . any deception (whether intentional or reckless) by words or conduct as to fact or as to law, including a deception as to the present intentions of the person using the deception or any other person."

the Act were in respect of the offences of robbery, burglary, aggravated burglary, blackmail and the replacement of receiving stolen goods by handling stolen property. Whilst it is beyond the scope of this work to examine the Theft Act 1968[67] it should be noted that its implementation has not been without problems, nor has it been uncontroversial. In particular, reference can be made to the difficulties involved in the interpretation of "appropriation" and "dishonesty".[68] It should not be presumed that the Act provides a model which is more efficient than the Larceny Act 1916 nor that it would accurately reflect Irish social views on dishonesty and its punishment.

192   But even if it is concluded that the Larceny Act 1916 provides the more appropriate model for Ireland that is not to say that the law is not in need of reform. It would seem to be quite obvious that the style in which the Act was drafted reflects the concerns of a pre-Independence draftsman. References to governmental structures which existed then are no longer appropriate and ought to be replaced; it is ironic that the expression "any of His Majesty's castles, palaces and houses"[69] remains in Irish law when His Majesty has long ceased to have castles, palaces or houses in this jurisdiction. The problem, in this respect, is that references to the Crown cannot be assumed to have been adapted either expressly or by implication, as in constitutional theory the State is not the successor of the Crown.[70] Royal invocations aside, the Act is drafted in the verbose and expansive style of the last century and could be altered to reflect contemporary drafting-style. A related point is that the system of aggravated punishments for larceny committed in different circumstances can be questioned. These are principally the legacy of the social concerns of a bygone era and their continued existence does not necessarily meet current social demands. Can it be said that the larceny of wills is of such gravity that it deserves penal servitude for life, while the larceny of documents of title attracts a comparatively light five years' penal servitude? As a matter of policy it might be preferable to have a single comprehensive offence of larceny, with a maximum penalty of, perhaps, ten years, and leave the selection of the appropriate sentence

67 For a commentary on English theft law see Smith, *The Law of Theft* (London, 1984) and Griew, *The Theft Acts 1968 and 1978* (London, 1986); see also Samuels, "Reform of the Law of Theft" (1968) 3 Ir. Jur. (n.s.) 273.

68 *Ibid.*; see e.g. *R v Morris* [1984] A.C. 320; *R v Feely* [1973] Q.B. 530; *R v McIvor* [1982] 1 All E.R. 491; *R v Ghosh* [1982] Q.B. 1053.

69 See section 7.

70 *Byrne v Ireland* [1972] I.R. 241.

to the discretion of the trial judge. Alternatively, if differential punishments are to be retained a schedule of punishments for the various forms of larceny could be incorporated into the Act. Likewise, a single comprehensive offence of extortion could well replace the cumbersome provisions of sections 29 to 31.[71]

193   Consideration might also be given to the creation of new offences which penalise certain forms of dishonesty whose position under the existing law is uncertain. In particular, although the law has traditionally been reluctant to criminalise the dishonest evasion of debts, some forms of debt evasion are morally and socially little different from larceny. Absconding without payment, popularly known as a "runner", is one case. If the accused intended at the outset to abscond he would be guilty of obtaining by false pretences; it is unlikely to be larceny by a trick as the restaurateur who provides the meal surely intends to pass title.[72] However, if the accused obtains the meal innocently and later decides to evade payment he is not guilty of an offence. Given the difficulty involved in establishing that the accused had the required intent at the outset an offence similar to the English offence of making off without payment[73] might be thought appropriate. A second case is the dishonest acquisition of services, or of a person's labour, which is unprovided for by the Act. In some cases the accused might be guilty of obtaining credit by fraud[74] but the mischief surely is that the victim is deprived of his labour which is not the concern of that offence. A third case is the unauthorised use of credit cards or cheque cards. There is some authority that such conduct amounts to a false pretence.[75] However, in that case it is not certain that the trader is induced to deal by the false representation that the accused is authorised to use the card and therefore, that the accused obtained by the false pretence; the accused's credit-worthiness is largely immaterial to the trader who deals because the presentation of the card amounts to a guarantee that the bank will honour the debt. To avoid these difficulties an offence which

71 See paras 125-142 *supra*.
72 Which distinguishes obtaining by false pretences from larceny by a trick; see paras 49-50 and 143 *supra*.
73 See s. 3 of the Theft Act 1978.
74 S. 13(1) of the Debtors (Ireland) Act 1872.
75 *R v Lambie* [1982] A.C. 449.

penalises the unauthorised use of a credit card might be necessary.[76] A fourth case is that of computer fraud. Given the difficulty involved in establishing a "taking" or "obtaining" or "conversion" special provision might be considered desirable for that activity.

76 Credit card legislation has been enacted in a number of American jurisdictions; see LaFave & Scott, *Criminal Law* (St Paul, Minn, 1972) p 672.

Schedule

Enactments Repealed

Session and Chapter	Title or Short Title	Extent of Repeal
33 Hen. 8, c. 12.		Section thirteen.
6 & 7 Vict. c. 96.	The Libel Act, 1843	Section three.
14 & 15 Vict. c. 100	The Criminal Procedure Act, 1851.	In section five, so far as it relates to Ireland, the words "stealing", "embezzling," and the words "or for obtaining by false pretences." Section eighteen, from the words "and in cases" to the end of the section.
17 & 18 Vict. c. 112.	The Literary and Scientific Institutions Act, 1854.	In section twenty-six, from "steal" to "chattels of institution, or."
23 & 24 Vict. c. 16.	The Municipal Corporation Mortgages, &c. Act, 1860.	Section seven.
24 & 25 Vict. c. 96.	The Larceny Act, 1861	In section one, from "the term 'trustee'" to "bankruptcy or insolvency"; and from "for the purposes of this Act, the night" to "succeeding day." Sections two to eleven, both inclusive. In section eighteen, from "and whosoever" to the end of the section. In section nineteen, from "and whosoever" to the end of the section. Section twenty. In section twenty-six, from the beginning of the section to "simple larceny and." In section twenty-seven, the words, "shall steal, or." In section twenty-eight, the words "shall steal, or." In section twenty-nine, the words, "steal or." In section thirty, the words "shall steal or." Sections thirty-one and thirty-two. In section thirty-three, from "and whosoever having been twice convicted" to the end of the section.

Schedule

Session and Chapter.	Title or Short Title.	Extent of Repeal.
24 & 25 Vict c. 96 — contd.		In section thirty-six, from "and whosoever" to the end of the section.
		Section thirty-eight.
		Sections forty to sixty-four, both inclusive.
		Sections sixty-seven to seventy-four, both inclusive.
		Sections seventy-seven to eighty-one both inclusive.
		Sections eighty-eight to ninety-six, both inclusive.
		In section ninety-eight, the words "except only a receiver of stolen property."
		Section one hundred and one hundred and one.
		Section one hundred and fourteen.
30 & 31 Vict. c. 35.	The Criminal Law Amendment Act, 1867.	In section nine, the words "either" and the words "or otherwise."
31 & 32 Vict. c. 116.	The Larceny Act, 1868	Section one.
34 & 35 Vict. c. 112.	The Prevention of Crimes Act, 1871.	Sections sixteen and nineteen.
39 & 40 Vict. c. 20.	The Statute Law Revision (Substituted Enactments) Act, 1876.	Section three.
45 & 46 Vict. c. 50.	The Municipal Corporations Act, 1882.	Section one hundred and seventeen.
45 & 46 Vict. c. 56.	The Electric Lighting Act, 1882.	Section twenty-three.
59 & 60 Vict. c. 52	The Larceny Act, 1896	The whole Act.
59 & 60 Vict. c. 57	The Burglary Act, 1896	The whole Act.
1 Edw. 7. c. 10	The Larceny Act, 1901	The whole Act.
4 & 5 Geo. 5. c. 58.	The Criminal Justice Administration Act, 1914.	Section thirty-five.
		Section thirty-nine, subsection two.
		The Third Schedule.

Index